The Practice of Value

The Berkeley Tanner Lectures

The Tanner Lectures on Human Values, which honour the American scholar, industrialist, and philanthropist Obert Clark Tanner, are presented annually at each of nine universities in the United States and England. They were established at the University of California, Berkeley, beginning in the 2000/1 academic year. This volume inaugurates a series of books based on the Berkeley Tanner Lectures. In this volume we include the lectures that Joseph Raz presented in March 2001, along with the responses of the three invited commentators on that occasion—Christine Korsgaard, Robert Pippin, and Bernard Williams—and a final rejoinder by Professor Raz. The volume is edited by Jay Wallace, who also contributes an Introduction. We have established the Berkeley Tanner Lectures Series in the belief that these distinguished lectures, together with the lively debates stimulated by their presentation in Berkeley, deserve to be made available to a wider audience. Additional volumes, based on the 2001/2 Tanner Lectures of Frank Kermode and the 2002/3 Tanner Lectures of Derek Parfit, are now in preparation.

ROBERT POST
SAMUEL SCHEFFLER
Series Editors

The Practice of Value

JOSEPH RAZ

With Commentaries by
CHRISTINE M. KORSGAARD
ROBERT PIPPIN
BERNARD WILLIAMS

Edited and Introduced by
R. JAY WALLACE

CLARENDON PRESS · OXFORD

*This book has been printed digitally and produced in a standard specification
in order to ensure its continuing availability*

OXFORD
UNIVERSITY PRESS

Great Clarendon Street, Oxford OX2 6DP

Oxford University Press is a department of the University of Oxford.
It furthers the University's objective of excellence in research, scholarship,
and education by publishing worldwide in

Oxford New York

Auckland Cape Town Dar es Salaam Hong Kong Karachi
Kuala Lumpur Madrid Melbourne Mexico City Nairobi
New Delhi Shanghai Taipei Toronto
With offices in
Argentina Austria Brazil Chile Czech Republic France Greece
Guatemala Hungary Italy Japan South Korea Poland Portugal
Singapore Switzerland Thailand Turkey Ukraine Vietnam

Oxford is a registered trade mark of Oxford University Press
in the UK and in certain other countries

Published in the United States
by Oxford University Press Inc., New York

ISBN 978-0-19-927846-6

Contents

REPLY TO COMMENTATORS

List of Contributors

CHRISTINE M. KORSGAARD is the Arthur Kingsley Porter Professor of Philosophy at Harvard University. She is the author of *The Sources of Normativity* (1996), which is an expanded version of her 1992 Tanner Lectures, and *Creating the Kingdom of Ends* (1996).

ROBERT PIPPIN is the Raymond W. and Martha Hilpert Gruner Distinguished Service Professor in the Committee on Social Thought, the Department of Philosophy, and the College at the University of Chicago. His books include *Henry James and Modern Moral Life* (2000), *Modernism as a Philosophical Problem* (1999), and *Idealism as Modernism* (1997). He is currently working on a book entitled *The Realization of Freedom: Hegel's Practical Philosophy*.

JOSEPH RAZ is Professor of the Philosophy of Law and a Fellow of Balliol College at the University of Oxford, and Professor at Columbia University. His numerous publications include *Value, Respect, and Attachment* (2001), *Engaging Reason* (2000), *Ethics in the Public Domain* (1995), *The Morality of Freedom* (1986), *The Authority of Law* (1979), *Practical Reason and Norms* (1975), and *The Concept of a Legal System* (1970).

R. JAY WALLACE is Professor of Philosophy at the University of California, Berkeley. He is the author of *Responsibility and the Moral Sentiments* (1994) and numerous papers in moral philosophy, and edited the collection *Reason, Emotion and Will* (1999).

BERNARD WILLIAMS is the Monroe Deutsch Professor of Philosophy at the University of California, Berkeley, and a Fellow of All Souls College, Oxford. His books include *Truth and Truthfulness*

(2002), *Shame and Necessity* (1993), *Making Sense of Humanity* (1995), *Ethics and the Limits of Philosophy* (1985), *Moral Luck* (1981), *Problems of the Self* (1973), *Utilitarianism: For and Against* (1973), and *Morality: An Introduction to Ethics* (1972).

Introduction

R. JAY WALLACE

It is hard to deny that our evaluative experiences—both what we value, and the ways in which we value things—are profoundly shaped by social practices. Many of the objects and activities that we esteem would not so much as exist in the absence of various contingent social and historical conditions. We could hardly be said to value philosophy, or romantic comedy, or textiles of the Arts and Crafts movement, in a social world that did not contain the quite distinctive forms of human activity necessary to produce instances of these genres. More generally, the ways in which we relate to valuable objects and undertakings, and the significance they have for our lives, themselves depend crucially on the social conditions under which we live. The beauty of a beautiful sunset may not depend on the contingent practices of human communities. But our access to this form of value is shaped by our culture, including the conceptual resources it makes available for thinking about the aesthetic dimensions of the natural world. Furthermore, the significance of natural beauty for human lives depends on its connection to a range of concrete cultural practices, such as those of romantic painting and poetry.

Joseph Raz's subject in *The Practice of Value* is the dependence of value on social practice. His views on this topic were delivered as the Tanner Lectures on Human Values at the University of California, Berkeley, in March 2001. The campus was fortunate to have commentaries on Raz's Tanner Lectures presented by three distinguished philosophers who take interestingly divergent approaches to issues in moral and social philosophy: Christine Korsgaard, Robert Pippin, and Bernard Williams. This book presents the revised text of Raz's Tanner Lectures, along with the replies by Korsgaard, Pippin, and Williams, and a new response to the replies by Raz. Together the contributions of these four philosophers constitute a fascinating debate about the relations between human values and the conditions under which human valuers live. At issue are not the contours of some specific value or set of values, but the perfectly general question of the historical and cultural presuppositions of evaluative experience and its objects. For all its abstraction, this is an issue that is of fundamental and ramifying importance not only for the theory of value, but more basically for human life, touching on questions that are of vital interest to us all.

Raz's reflections are an attempt to come to grips with 'the contingency at the heart of value' (p. 59). He takes as his starting point the kinds of observations offered above, about the ways in which social practices seem to shape our activities as valuers. Raz is deeply impressed by the apparent dependence of values on the historical and cultural conditions that give rise to them. The difficulty is to account for this kind of dependence in a way that does justice to the range and complexity of our evaluative practices. In particular, Raz is concerned to make sense of the social dependence of value without falling back on a kind of cultural relativism, according to which the application of value concepts is restricted to the social conditions that originally produced them and that continue to sustain them. If values depend on social practices, how can we deploy them to make judgements about persons, actions, and objects that exist outside the relevant practices? Should we not suppose that the dependence of value on social practice entails a contraction of the range of our value judgements?

Raz thinks not. His defence of the social dependence of values takes the form of a sustained argument for two distinct theses. The *special social dependence thesis* holds that some values exist only if there are (or were) social practices sustaining them. The *general social dependence thesis* asserts that nearly all values depend in one way or another on social practices: either by being subject to the special dependence thesis, or through their dependence on other values that are subject to that thesis. As Raz interprets and develops these claims, they do not entail a general relativistic restriction in the scope of evaluative assessment. For one thing, there are a number of values that escape the net of the special dependence thesis, and that can therefore exist independently of social practices that take some particular shape. These include pure sensual and perceptual pleasures; the aesthetic values of natural phenomena (such as the beauty and grandeur of a landscape); such enabling or facilitating moral values as freedom; and the value of people. To the extent these values can exist independently of particular social and historical conditions, we can straightforwardly apply them to make value judgements in a way that is unconstrained by historical and social contingency. The basic value of persons, whatever it might amount to, is a value that is instantiated wherever persons exist, regardless of the historical or social conditions under which they live. Even in regard to values that are subject to the special dependence thesis, moreover, their dependence on social practices does not in Raz's view entail a relativistic restriction in the scope of their application. Raz contends that 'once a value comes into being, it bears on everything, without restriction' (p. 22). The social and historical factors that condition the emergence of values of this kind, in other words, do not prevent us from appealing to them as extensively as we may need to as we make our way through the world.

But if values can function in this way as non-relativistic standards for assessment, why contend that they are dependent on social practices? What fundamentally motivates this central claim? Take first the 'cultural' values to which the special dependence thesis primarily applies, such as the values embodied in film, opera, literature, and philosophy. Raz's guiding thought about examples of these kinds seems to be that the values in question represent combinations of specific value properties, and that if we abstract completely from contingent historical and cultural conditions, there is no reason to favour one way of combining those properties over others that are equally possible. Cultural evaluation is typically 'genre based': in judging a film to be (say) a good romantic comedy, we will be guided by our understanding of the genre to which the film belongs, which fixes the combinations of evaluative properties that are looked for in a successful instance of the genre. But genres are themselves products of quite specific and contingent historical and social conditions, and this gives a clear sense to the suggestion that cultural values depend on social practices. In the absence of the appropriate social conditions there would simply not be anything that is good in the way that is distinctive of romantic comedies or neoclassical architecture. The special ways in which concrete evaluative properties are mixed or combined in these cases could not guide assessment if there were not a social practice that established such combinations as worthy of pursuit and appreciation. Once a cultural value has come into existence it can be sustained, revived, and applied independently of particular social practices; but the right kinds of social practices are necessary for making evaluation in terms of specific cultural values possible in the first place.

With other kinds of value the relation to social practices takes on a rather different form. Here it is not so much that the values would not exist in the absence of certain social conditions, but that they derive their point and purpose from their relation to the kinds of cultural values to which the special dependence thesis applies. Thus such 'enabling' moral values as freedom and fidelity are significant precisely because they make it possible for people to pursue and engage with a range of first-order goods, including the cultural values to which the special dependence thesis applies. To the extent this is the case, the point of these enabling values depends on certain social practices—namely, those that condition the concrete goods whose pursuit the enabling values make possible. Similarly, the value of persons is not something that depends for its existence on particular social practices. But what is valuable about persons is precisely their capacity to appreciate and respond to the good, so the point of this capacity can be realized fully only in relation to the kinds of concrete value that are directly dependent on social and cultural practices.

This line of argument does not apply to such values as sensual and perceptual pleasure, or to the aesthetic values instantiated in natural objects (the beauty of a mountain vista). It would be odd to say that the point of these values depends on the kinds of cultural value that are covered by the special dependence thesis, and for this reason Raz introduces a minor qualification when he formulates the general dependence thesis, admitting that there may be some exceptions to it. But the significance of this qualification is diminished by the following considerations. First, some of the values that fall into this class of exceptions are values that exhibit a still different kind of dependence on social practices. Thus, the aesthetic qualities exhibited by nature may not depend for their existence or their point on specific cultural formations; but our *access* to values of these kinds is typically mediated by cultural formations, which provide us with distinctive resources for conceptualizing natural beauty, and make available concrete social practices that give the appreciation of this form of value an importance it would not otherwise exhibit. Furthermore, Raz makes the claim that the kinds of values that are capable of giving our lives meaning and purpose are exclusively values that are socially dependent in one way or another. Purely sensual and perceptual pleasures, considered merely as momentary experiences in the life of an organism, are not the kind of values that can supply us with reason to go on in life, and that provide an organizing focus for our planning and activity. Values acquire this kind of importance only when they are appropriately integrated within cultural practices. For this reason, 'the life-building values are socially dependent, directly or indirectly' (p. 36).

In the second part of his text Raz extends and elaborates his observations about the social dependence of value, focusing on the topics of pluralism, change, and understanding. He begins by noting the ways in which evaluation often depends on identification of an appropriate genre or kind, especially where the cultural values are concerned. In cases of this type, evaluative assessment typically proceeds in two stages: first we identify the genre to which an object, action, or performance belongs (is it a sonata, or an instance of modern dance?); then we ascertain whether the item is good or bad as an instance of the identified kind or genre. Evaluation can be tied to genre in this way even in cases in which an object of assessment stands in an unorthodox relation to prevailing standards (for example, as an ironic or eclectic exemplar of existing kinds). The fundamental point is that genre-based evaluation illustrates clearly the way in which value can depend on social practices without importing the danger of relativism. The dependence of genre on social practice gives a clear sense to the thesis that value itself depends on social practice: both the concrete items that exemplify genres, and the standards that govern their assessment, would not so much as exist in the absence of contingent social conditions. But once the relevant conditions are established, it may be a perfectly objective and determinate matter whether a given object is (say) an excellent exemplification of the sonata form, or of the conventions of modern dance.

The central role of genre in evaluative thought helps to make sense of a further thesis that is important to moral and political thinking, that of value pluralism. This thesis holds that there are many distinct values, not reducible to a single kind of value or way of being good, and that the distinct values may also be incapable of being realized together in the life of a single individual or society. Pluralism in this form is not exactly a consequence of the social dependence thesis, but the latter thesis does help us to understand the idea that there is a fundamental plurality of values. In particular, the relation of evaluation to genre suggests a natural model for the claim that there are distinct ways of being good. One set of legal arrangements might be valuable, for instance, as an instance of the adversarial system of criminal justice, whereas another set of arrangements is valuable as an instance of the prosecutorial system. Furthermore, the features of a given system that render it good in one of these ways might precisely prevent it from exhibiting the kind of value exemplified in arrangements of the other kind. There need be no contradiction in cases of this kind between our judgements that the two conflicting systems are both valuable, since those judgements are grounded in distinct genres.

Finally, Raz takes up questions regarding the epistemological implications of the dependence of value on social practice. A first point he makes is that our grasp of cultural values is best conceived as a form of complex understanding and judgement, as is appropriate to the 'dense texture' of cases that distinctively involve the mixing of a variety of component goods. Knowledge of this kind is often merely implicit, and it must be sustained and transmitted by the very practices that condition cultural values in the first place. But these same features of cultural values make disagreement and indeterminacy virtually inevitable: situations will arise in which people who are acquainted with the relevant sustaining cultural practices and institutions come to conflicting conclusions about whether a given exemplar (a new novel or dance performance, say) is excellent and successful, as an instance of its genre. Raz rejects the subjectivist inference from persistent disagreement to the conclusion that all conflicts of value judgement represent mere differences in taste. Intractable local disagreement about value takes place against the background of substantial agreement, and is indeed made possible by such agreement. Nor will it do to treat local disagreements either as reflections of ignorance regarding the precise contours of our value concepts, or as the result of localized vagueness in those concepts, which the parties to the dispute could simply acknowledge and accept.

Instead, Raz defends the surprising claim that rival and incompatible accounts of the application of cultural values can *both* be correct. This is the right thing to say in cases in which the social practices that sustain a cultural value underdetermine that value, leaving it essentially unclear which particular standard of excellence is appropriate for resolving questions about the application of the value. A helpful concept for making sense of evaluative knowledge under these conditions is the concept of interpretation. Interpretations are governed by objective standards (there is such a thing as mistaken or misguided interpretations), but in a way that allows for a variety of divergent but equally worthy or successful interpretations that each reflect the personality and temperament of the interpreter. Interpretative understanding can thus be both objectively constrained and expressive at the same time, and Raz suggests that this provides a good model for thinking about our knowledge of the cultural values that are most directly dependent on social practices. To make sense of evaluative understanding, we must move beyond the simple dichotomy between an objective realm of thought that is free from indeterminacy and ambiguity, and domains in which thinking is entirely a subjective matter of taste. We can have more evaluative knowledge than subjectivists and sceptics have tended to countenance, but such knowledge as we attain about the good exhibits distinctive features that reflect the dependence of value on social practices and the forms of indeterminacy that stem from that dependence.

Raz's commentators offer critical responses to his account of the relation between value and practice from strikingly different philosophical perspectives. Christine Korsgaard questions whether we can really make sense of the idea that values depend on social practices. Certain valuable objects, to be sure, are such that they would presumably not exist in the absence of appropriate social practices and traditions. But it does not follow that the values exemplified in these objects are themselves socially dependent. Korsgaard places in the centre of her account of value the activity of valuing, an activity engaged in by human agents, and subject to determinate and perfectly objective constraints. To be valuable is fundamentally to be something that it would be *appropriate* for an agent to value. But the standards that determine when and in what ways it would be appropriate to value a given object are specified not by social practices, but by the nature both of the object to be valued and of the person engaged in the activity of evaluative reflection. Among the norms that govern our activity as valuers are the very norms that determine the identity of the objects of evaluative consideration. Thus, something or someone might satisfy fully the standards of excellence enshrined in a given genre, without yet being on that account good. The good prefabricated tract house, for instance, is not necessarily good as an example of the kind of thing that it most essentially is, since it may not achieve the purposes that are partly built into the very concept of a human habitation, and that define objects as instances of this concept. Korsgaard suggests that it is the nature of valuers as human that is the ultimate source of values, fixing the most important constraints on what we can appropriately value.

Korsgaard challenges Raz from a point of view that draws broadly on Aristotle and Kant, suggesting that values depend not on culture but on nature (including above all our human nature). Robert Pippin, by contrast, takes seriously Raz's observations about the social dependence of value, but questions whether he has succeeded in resisting the potentially relativistic implications of social dependence. Pippin finds attractive the combination of social dependence and objectivity in Raz's treatment of value. But he wonders whether the right kind of objectivity can be upheld once we have fully assimilated the lesson that values depend on contingent social and historical practices. Raz relies on a distinction between the social conditions for the existence of particular values, and the normative resources we call on for establishing first-order conclusions about the good. The fact that a given way of combining or mixing properties is valued by the members of some historical community may be necessary for the existence of the corresponding value. But we cannot establish that the relevant combinations are valuable simply by appealing to the social fact that they are valued by the members of the community. Beyond that, it is necessary to have 'recourse to the whole of [our] conceptual armoury, information, and powers of argumentation' (p. 25), including our normative concepts and judgements, to determine whether the valued objects really are good or not.

Against this, Pippin warns that the kinds of social dependence that Raz himself affirms threaten to undermine the autonomy and reliability of the conceptual and normative resources he would have us draw on to establish evaluative conclusions. In the absence of the kind of Aristotelian-cum-Kantian framework to which Korsgaard appeals, there is no guarantee that the normative judgements we reach in evaluative reflection are more than mere reflections of our contingent preferences and interests. Perhaps there is no practical alternative to relying on our own normative concepts and categories when we think about concrete evaluative issues. But this does not show that those resources are in good order, or that they enable us to arrive at true judgements about what is and is not genuinely valuable. Furthermore, Raz's reflections about the inevitability of disagreement in interpretative reasoning about the good seem potentially to reinforce these kinds of worries. The persistence and depth of these disagreements, concerning some of the most central and important concepts of contemporary moral and political life (such as the right to life, or to equal consideration under the law), can easily make a relativistic or sceptical understanding of the original disputes seem attractive. In the end, Pippin suggests that Raz's acknowledgement of the social contingency of our evaluative practices has implications for the status and meaning of our first-order normative thought that Raz himself has not fully come to terms with.

Bernard Williams shares Pippin's suspicion that we cannot fully insulate evaluative enquiry from our awareness of the historical and social contingency of our evaluative practices. At the same time, he agrees with Raz that a generalized relativism is the wrong response to this awareness. Williams poses the question of whether, in the attempt to arrive at a more satisfactory understanding of the implications of social contingency, it is really helpful to formulate the issue in the ontological terms Raz prefers, as an issue about the *existence* of values. In the case of values that are not dependent on social practices, such as the beauty of the natural world, we shall have to say that the relevant value existed even before people came around to recognizing and appreciating it. But this invites us to think about the historical processes through which the beauty of nature came to be acknowledged as the overcoming of a cognitive deficiency of some kind, and Williams suggests that this is not the most fruitful and illuminating framework for thinking about those processes. Similar difficulties arise, Williams suggests, when we turn to the cultural values to which the social dependence thesis most directly pertains. Once these come into existence, Raz wants to say that they apply to everything, without restriction. But—to take an especially central example—if the values of political liberalism did not yet exist in the Middle Ages, it is hard to see how it could have been a failing or a deficiency of the societies then existing that they did not (say) honour the equal rights of women. And if it was neither a failing nor a deficiency in the earlier societies that they did not realize or even aspire to liberal ideals in this way, it becomes correspondingly unclear what it might mean to say that those values apply to the earlier society.

Williams himself suggests that there is often little point to criticizing earlier societies by appeal to our own contemporary political and social values. We would need the kind of Aristotelian framework that Korsgaard adumbrates to make sense of the claim that it is a failing or deficiency in the earlier societies that they did not do very well by the standards of political liberalism. But Williams is notably more sceptical than Korsgaard about the prospects for Aristotelian teleology in the modern world. Moreover, he believes that our consciousness of the resulting contingency of value cannot help but impinge on our first-order evaluative thought. The task faced by both theory and practice is to find a way of confronting this historical and social contingency, without losing confidence in what are after all the only values we have.

Raz's response to the commentators is exceptionally wide-ranging, and extends and clarifies his views on a host of important issues. I shall not attempt to summarize his many points, except to mention one theme that is relevant to all the commentaries, and that emerges with especial clarity in Raz's response. This concerns the role of evaluative concepts and judgements in philosophical theorizing about both the nature and the objects of evaluative thought. Reflecting on his most general methodological commitments in the lectures, Raz affirms that 'we need to employ all the evaluative/ normative concepts at our disposal, and resort to many of their essential properties, to understand and establish the nature of any of them, and to establish the nature of what is good or bad' (p. 148). As against Korsgaard, he rejects the idea that we must provide a philosophical vindication of our normative categories—tracing them to their 'source'—before we are entitled to rely on them in philosophical reflection and practical deliberation. But he rejects equally the claim of Pippin and Williams that awareness of the contingency of our evaluative practices must inevitably affect our first-order normative reflection. Whether it does this or not, I believe Raz would say, will have to be decided on a case-by-case basis, by looking at particular examples of historical and social contingency, and drawing on the totality of our conceptual and normative resources to establish what we should say about the concrete implications of the kind of contingency that has been uncovered. This is the holistic method that Raz himself deploys in reaching his conclusion that the social dependence of value does not commit us to relativism, and his lectures present an excellent illustration of its potential to illuminate the larger landscape of value.

The Practice of Value

JOSEPH RAZ

The Thesis

Social Dependence without Relativism

The Landscape

'Man is the measure of all things; of what is, that it is; of what is not, that it is not,' said Protagoras, launching one of those philosophical ideas that reverberate through the centuries, acquiring meanings of their own, or providing inspiration for various doctrines, some quite removed from their originator's. 'Man is the measure' is such an idea, a thought that many, not only philosophers, find irresistible, while others find in it nothing but confusion.

Even though I will not follow Protagoras' views,[1] the spirit of his maxim will hover over these lectures. My concern, though, will not be with all things. Only the value or disvalue of things. Is Man the measure of value? Clearly not, where what is of instrumental value only is concerned. Things are of mere instrumental value when their

I presented early drafts of material out of which the lectures were carved at a seminar I gave in Oxford in Hilary Term 2001, and at a visit to Ann Arbor as a Nelson Philosopher in Residence. I am grateful to participants in these sessions, and in particular to Peter Railton, Thomas Hofweber, Eric Lormand, Allan Gibbard, Liz Anderson, David Velleman, and Adam Morton. Of the many people whose questions or observations during the discussions and in private conversations following the lectures were helpful in writing the reply I would like to thank in particular Jay Wallace, Tamar Schapiro, and Barry Stroud. I discussed early drafts of both lectures and replies with Ulrike Heuer, the influence of whose criticism, our continuing disagreements notwithstanding, can be found throughout.

[1] Whose interpretation is in dispute. He is taken to be a subjectivist, believing that whatever one believes is true for one, or an objectivist, holding that whatever anyone believes is true, or (by Plato in *Theaetetus* 177b) a relativist, holding that whatever the city decides is just is just in the city. I will not be tempted by any of them.

value is entirely due to the value of what they bring about, or to the value of what they are likely to bring about or may be used to bring about. The instrumental value of things is at least in part a product of how things are in the world, of the causal powers of things. These lectures will consider the case for thinking that Man is the measure of intrinsic value. This narrows the field considerably. For example, the value of the means of personal survival, such as food, shelter, good health, is merely instrumental.[2]

In matters evaluative, Protagoras' maxim seems to dominate our horizon. Its triumph seems to have been the gift, or the price, depending on your point of view, of secularism, and of the rise of a world view dominated by the physical sciences. But in what way exactly do values depend on us? That is not a straightforward question, and the history of philosophy is littered with a vast array of very different answers.

The view I will explore is most closely related to social relativism, which I reject, and to value pluralism, which I accept. I will emphasize my difference with the first in this lecture, and my debt to the second in the lecture to follow. Social relativism, holding that the merit or demerit of actions and other objects of evaluation is relative to the society in which they take place or in which they are judged, is a popular view. Indeed some mild forms of it cannot be denied. Who would deny that in Rome one should behave as the Romans do, at least on a natural understanding of this view, which, among other things, does not take the maxim itself to be socially relative. Such partial or moderate social relativism is surely true in some form or another, and yet it is too tame to do justice to Protagoras' maxim. True, it can take a thorough form, generalizing the Roman maxim (normally understood to have restricted application to some kinds of matter only) to all actions, taking the value or rightness of any action to be a function of, say, the practices in its locality. But even so, local

---

[2] That is qua means of survival their value is merely instrumental. Those same things may also have value for other reasons.

relativism[3] is not relativistic through and through. Local standards, those that bind only members of some community, are so binding because they are validated by universal principles, not themselves relativistic. Thoroughgoing local relativism makes the application of all non-relative standards be mediated by others that are socially dependent, and therefore relativistic. But it is still local relativism, in being moored in universal and socially independent principles of value.[4] It does not hold that Man is the measure of all value. Some values remain socially independent, and those that are socially dependent are so because of them.

Radical social relativism goes further. It not only makes the value or rightness of action depend on social factors, it makes all evaluative standards socially relative: they are valid only where they are prac-tised, or they are subject to some other social condition. Radical social relativism risks contradiction, for it has to explain whether the claim that all value is socially relative is itself socially relative.[5]

Some thoroughgoing varieties of relativism escape contradiction; radical relativism might, for instance, be presented as a form of per-spectival relativism, holding truth to be truth in or relative to some

[3] I use the expression 'local relativism' to indicate forms of relativism in which (a) the rightness or value of at least some actions is determined by norms that make it dependent on the practices of the place where they were performed or where they are judged; and which (b) include norms whose validity is universal, i.e. they apply time-lessly, or to all times and all places. Thoroughgoing local relativism makes the value and rightness of all actions a function of some social practices, but the norms that determine that that is so, or at any rate some of them, are not themselves relative.

[4] These characterizations are precise enough for their purpose here, but admitted-ly they leave much unclear, much room for further distinctions. My purpose below is to exploit this unclarity to advance the view I find more promising, which can be regarded as either a special variant of local or of radical relativism, or as different from both.

[5] The argument is that, if it is not, then radical social relativism is false, for at least one standard of value, this one, is not socially relative. If it is socially relative, then it is true, but only locally, relative to some societies or some perspectives, and therefore radical relativism is false because it is false that necessarily any standard is true only relative to a society or a perspective. If the standard that says so is nowhere accepted then no standard is relative.

perspectives.[6] But other problems remain. Radical relativism is charged with making it impossible for us to have the opinions we think we have. We take some of our views to be true absolutely, and not qualified by being relative to a perspective. Similarly, certain disagreements that we believe we have with others turn out either not to be disagreements at all, or to have a character very different from what we thought they had.

How damaging this point is to radical relativism is a moot question. Radical relativism is a response to a felt crisis that undermines our confidence in evaluative thought due to the persistence of irresolvable disagreements, and other chronic diseases of evaluative thought. Its cure is to reinterpret evaluative thought preserving much of it, but changing it enough to rid it of its ailments. To complain that the remedy involves change is somewhat ungracious. How else is it meant to work?

And yet the reforming aspect of perspectival relativism makes it an option of last resort. It is a response to a perception of a host of insoluble problems that bedevil evaluative thought, and require its reform. What if the problems are illusory? What if their perception is a result of a blinkered theoretical understanding or, rather, misunderstanding of the phenomena? In that case we do not need the cure, with its prescribed amputation of aspects of our evaluative thought. Indeed, we should avoid it as a distortion of a healthy practice.

I will argue for social dependence without relativism—that is, for the view that values, and therefore also reasons, rights, virtues, and other normative phenomena, that depend on them, are socially dependent, but in a way that does not involve radical relativism, that does not imply that what is valuable is valuable only in societies that think that it is, nor that evaluative or normative concepts, or the truth of propositions about them, are relative.

It would be pleasing to be able to say that unlike relativism the view I will explore explains evaluative thinking without reforming

---

[6] See, for one example, S. D. Hales, 'A Consistent Relativism', *Mind*, 106 (1997), 33–52.

it. But that is not quite so. My hope is, however, that we can dissociate the social dependence of value from relativism, and that in doing so we are better able to explain the basic features of evaluative thinking. The suggestion is that most of what social and perspectival relativism promises to explain is explained by the social dependence of value. Radical relativism is detachable from the thesis of social dependence, and adds no merit to it. We can settle for the less radical and less revisionary view I offer, and remain more faithful to the basic features of our evaluative thinking.[7]

THE THESIS IN BRIEF

The Thesis

It is time to put some flesh on the enigmatic remarks made so far. The social dependence of values, or at least the aspect of it that concerns me, can be expressed as the combination of two theses:

- *The special social dependence thesis* claims that some values exist only if there are (or were) social practices sustaining them.
- *The (general) social dependence thesis* claims that, with some exceptions, all values depend on social practices either by being subject to the special thesis or through their dependence on values that are subject to the special thesis.

This formulation is vague in various ways. In particular it does little to identify which values are and which are not subject to the theses. I will consider later the reach of the two theses. But first, let us dwell on the special thesis for a moment, using the sort of examples of which it is most likely to be true, without worrying about its reach.

---

[7] A word of clarification: I introduced the lecture by contrasting my view, which follows, with relativism. I do not, however, intend to follow with a critique of relativism. The difficulties with relativism have been ably discussed by various writers. My purpose is to expound the virtues of my account of the social dependence of value. I introduce it by highlighting the ways it differs from relativism to pre-empt any misunderstanding of it as a form of relativism.

Regarding any value, there is in any population *a sustaining practice* if people conduct themselves approximately as they would were they to be aware of it, and if they do so out of (an openly avowed) belief that it is worthwhile to conduct themselves as they do (under some description or another).

I identify sustaining practices in this way to allow that the people engaging in them may not be aware of the value their conduct is sustaining, or that they have only a dim and imperfect knowledge of it, or that they mistake it for something else, which is in fact of no value at all, but which leads them to the same conduct to which the value in question, had it been known to them, would have led them. At the same time, sustaining practices cannot consist merely of conduct identical, or close, to the one that the value would lead one to adopt. This coincidence cannot be purely arbitrary. It must result at least from belief in the value of such conduct.

It may be objected that to count as sustaining a value those whose practice it is must have that value as their reason to engage in the practice. This objection misconceives the nature of the thesis. It does not explain some intuitive notion of a sustaining practice. We have only the vaguest intuitive grasp of that notion, and I am using it in a regimented form to make a theoretical point.

The reasons why the weaker condition that I stipulated seems the better one are three. First, it avoids the awkward question of how adequate people's grasp of the nature of the value must be before their practice can be regarded as sustaining it. The difficulty is not that any attempt to set such a test would be vague. The difficulty is that for the purpose of relating value to practice there is no reason to expect a good understanding of the nature of the value. We cannot expect people to come to a correct view of its nature by examining the practice.[8] Therefore, while practices entail common knowledge of their terms—that is, of what they require—we need not expect the

---

[8] See below, 'Dependence without Conventionalism'.

practices to be informed by a good understanding of the values that could justify or make sense of them.

Second, more general values are put into practice through more specific ones, as when we express our respect for freedom by adherence to the value of the rule of law, among others. While I will not discuss these matters in detail, I share the view that it makes sense to say that a culture or civilization, or country, respected a general value on the ground that it recognized and sustained in practice many of the more specific values that implement it in the conditions there prevailing. That may be so even if they did not have the concept of the more general value. And if so, it becomes necessary to allow that the sustaining practices of the more specific values sustain the more general one, which they manifest.

Third, as we shall see, values are open to reinterpretation, and to leave that possibility open while maintaining the social dependence thesis we need to leave the relation between value and practice fairly loose and flexible, otherwise the practice will block too many possible reinterpretations.[9]

The examples of opera, intimate friendships, and others show that most often the practices will relate to a set of interrelated values. One may not be able to identify separately practices relating to singing, conducting, and so on in operas. The sustaining practices that consist of attending operas, music school, listening to CDs, discussing them, writing and reading about them, and so on relate to various aspects of the art, some of which may be related more directly to one or more practices, but which still derive sustenance from all of them.

The dependence of value on practice that the thesis affirms is not simultaneous and continuous. The thesis is that the existence of values depends on the existence of sustaining practices at some point, not that these practices must persist as long as the value does. The usual pattern is for the emergence, out of previous social forms, of a new set of practices, bringing into life a new form: monogamous

---

[9] See below, 'Interpretation', in 'Implications'.

marriage between partners chosen by each other, the opera, and so on, with their attendant excellences. Once they come into being, they remain in existence even if the sustaining practices die out. They can be known even if exclusively from records. They can get forgotten and be rediscovered, and the like. Their meaning may change with time, and I will return to this in the next lecture. Sometimes they are kept alive, as it were, by small groups of devotees. The important point is that once they are brought into being through an existing practice they need not ever be lost again, except accidentally, and that regardless of the passing-away of their sustaining practices.

You can see now why this form of social dependence does not involve social relativism. There is no suggestion that what is of value is so only in societies where the value is appreciated, nor that rights, duties, or virtues exist only where recognized. Once a value comes into being, it bears on everything, without restriction. But its existence has social preconditions.

The asymmetry between initial emergence and continued existence lies at the root of the special dependence thesis. It is entrenched in the way we think about cultural values: Greek tragedy was born in a nest of sustaining practices; neither it, nor the forms of excellence it brought with it, existed before. But they exist now, even though the attendant practices have long since disappeared. Moreover, the theoretical motivations for the social dependence thesis do not require continuous social support. For example, the existence and knowability of values can just as well be explained by reference to practices now defunct, and so can the dependence of values on realization through valuers. But I have gone ahead of myself. Before I turn to the justification of the thesis, a few more clarifications are necessary.

Dependence without Reduction

It is sometimes thought that social dependence is a normatively, or ethically, conservative thesis. Since it affirms that value depends on social practices, it must, it is concluded, approve of how things are, for according to it all the values by which we judge how things are derive from that very reality. This is a non-sequitur.

The first point to note is that bads as well as goods are, according to the social dependence thesis, dependent on social practices. The very same social practices that create friendships and their forms of excellence also create forms of disloyalty and betrayal, forms of abuse and exploitation.

If both goods and bads, both positive and negative values, are socially dependent, what determines whether what a practice sustains is a positive or a negative value? Do goods and bads have the character they have because they are taken by participants in the practice to have it? Not quite. The worry arises out of the thought that the social dependence thesis is reductive in nature. That is, it may be thought that it commits one to a two-step procedure: first one identifies a sustaining practice in value-free terms, and then one identifies, by reference to it, the character of the positive or negative value it sustains. Such a procedure seems to me hopeless. There is no way we can capture the variety and nuance of various concepts of values and disvalues except in evaluative terms—that is, by using some evaluative concepts to explain others. The social dependence thesis is not meant to provide any form of reductive explanation of concepts. Reductive explanations only distort the phenomena to be explained. Evaluative concepts provide ways of classifying events, things, and other matters by their evaluative significance. Non-evaluative classifications—even if they succeed, *per impossibile*, in bringing together everything, capable of being identified by non-evaluative criteria, that falls under an evaluative concept—cannot make sense of the reason they are classified together, nor can they sustain counterfactuals and determine what would belong together were things significantly other than they are.[10] Sustaining practices

---

[10] A point first explained by J. McDowell in 'Aesthetic Value, Objectivity, and the Fabric of the World', repr. in *Mind, Value, and Reality* (Cambridge, Mass.: Harvard University Press, 1998).

can be identified only in normative language, referring to the very values they sustain.

This claim appears neutral between the concepts of true and false values. That is, the claim is that value concepts are explained by reference, among other things, to other value concepts, and it seems not to matter whether the concepts used in the explanations are of true or of illusory or false values. But appearances are misleading. Concepts of false values cannot have instances. Schematically speaking, if there is no value V, then the concept of V is a concept of a false or illusory value and there is nothing that can have the value V (because there is no such value). We inevitably try to explain any concepts, whether we take them to be of what is real or of the illusory or impossible, by the use of concepts that can have instances. Concepts that cannot have instances do not connect the concepts they are used to explain to the world or to anything in it, and thus they fail to explain them. It is true that to explain the concept of an illusory value we need to point to its connections, should it have such, to other concepts of other illusory values. These concepts are likely to be part of a system of (incoherent, or flawed) beliefs, and to understand any of them we need to understand their interrelations. But, unless they are also related to concepts that can have instances, they remain unattached to anything real, and their understanding is locked in a circle of notions detached from anything possible. To have a better grasp of such concepts we need to relate them to concepts with possible instantiation at least by reference to their aspirations. That is, those concepts are taken to be, in earnest, in joke, or in fiction, related to something real and we need to understand these aspirational connections to understand the concepts.

Thus people's understanding of concepts generally, and value concepts are no exceptions, depends, among other things, on their understanding of their relations to concepts that can have instances. In the case of value concepts that means that it depends on their understanding of concepts of true values.[11] This establishes that the

[11] The implication is that, if people come to realize that their understanding of value concepts depends on concepts of false values (e.g. of religious values), they realize that

social dependence thesis is in no way a reductive thesis of evaluative concepts.

We can now see why the charge of conservatism is unjustified. The charge is that the special thesis entails acceptance of what people take to be good practices as good practices, and what they take to be bad practices as bad practices, that it is committed to accepting any practice of any kind of evaluative concept as defining a real good or a real bad, as its practioners take it to do. To which the answer is that it does not. The existence of a sustaining practice is merely a necessary, not a sufficient condition for the existence of some kinds of values. The special thesis does not in any way privilege the point of view of any group or culture. It allows one full recourse to the whole of one's conceptual armoury, information, and powers of argumentation in reaching conclusions as to which practices sustain goods and which sustain evil, or worthless things, which are, perhaps, taken to be good by a population.[12] Of course, deficiency in our conceptual, informational, and argumentational powers may well make us blind to some goods, or lead us to accept some evils. But that must be true in any case. The special dependence thesis would be to blame only if it denied that such limitations lead to mistakes, and privileged the concepts or information of some group or culture. But that it does not do.

Dependence without Conventionalism

Another objection to the social dependence thesis is that it turns all values into conventional values. However, this objection is based on

it is defective and has to be revised and reorientated by relating it to concepts of true values. I am inclined to believe that people who have value concepts necessarily have some concepts of true values. But there is no need to consider this question here. The remarks above about the priority of concepts with possible instances are consistent with recognition that people's understanding of concepts they possess can be, and normally is, incomplete. I discussed some of the issues involved in 'Two Views of the Nature of the Theory of Law: A Partial Comparison', *Legal Theory*, 4 (1998), 249–82 (at 261–73), repr. in J. Coleman, *Hart's Postscript* (Oxford: Oxford University Press, 2001).

[12] It also allows one to judge that some groups or cultures miss out on some goods, which are not known to them.

another unfounded assumption, that if the existence of a value depends on a sustaining practice that practice must be a reason for the value, a reason for why it is a value, or something like that. That is the case with conventional goods, which are goods the value of which derives, at least in part, from the fact that many people value them. I say 'at least in part', identifying conventional goods broadly, because this seems to me to conform better with the way we think of conventional goods. Few are purely conventional in the sense that nothing but the fact that people generally value them makes them valuable. Paradigmatically conventional goods, like the good of giving flowers as a mark of affection, have reasons other than the convention. The fragrance, colours, and shapes of flowers are appealing partly for independent reasons, and make them appropriate for their conventional role. Most commonly these independent grounds for valuing flowers are themselves culturally dependent; they are not, at least not entirely, a product of our biology. But the cultural dependence of our valuing of flowers because of their colours, shapes, and fragrance is not in itself of the right kind to make their value a conventional value. We would not value them had we not been imbued with culturally transmitted attitudes. But we do not think that the fact that others value them is a reason why lilies are beautiful. However, the fact that others think it appropriate to give flowers for birthdays makes them appropriate birthday presents.

Conventionalism should be distinguished from social dependence. Conventionalism is a normative doctrine, identifying the reasons making what is right or valuable right or valuable. On the other hand, social dependence is, if you like, a metaphysical thesis, about a necessary condition for the existence of (some) values. This does not mean that the existence of values is a brute fact, which cannot be explained. It can be explained in two complementary ways. On the one hand, there may be a historical explanation for the emergence and fate of the sustaining practices. Why did opera emerge when it did, and so on. On the other hand, there will be normative explanations of why operatic excellence is a genuine form of excellence. That explanation is, however, none other than the familiar explanation of why anything of value is of value: it points to the value of the form in combining music, dance, visual display, acting, and words, in providing a form for a heightened characterization of central human experiences, or whatever.

With these clarifications behind us, let us turn to the reasons for the social dependence thesis.

JUSTIFYING CONSIDERATIONS

The Dependence of Values on Valuers

Four considerations, or clusters of considerations, support the social dependence of values. (1) It offers a promising route towards an explanation of the existence of values. (2) It points to a ready explanation of how we can know about them. (3) It accounts for the deeply entrenched common belief that there is no point to value without valuers. No point to beauty without people, or other valuers, who can appreciate it. No point to the value of love without lovers. No point in the value of truth without potential knowers. (4) Finally, and most importantly, it fits the basic structures of our evaluative thinking.

All four considerations support the social dependence of value. None of them requires relativism. So far as they are concerned, radical relativism is to be embraced only if it is the inevitable result of the social dependence of value. But that, as we shall see, it is not.

The brief discussion that follows concentrates on the last two considerations, only occasionally touching on the others. Let me start with what I take to be the fundamental thought—namely, that values depend on valuers.

The thought is so familiar that it is difficult to catch it in words, difficult to express it accurately. It is also one that can be easily misunderstood and is often exaggerated. Perhaps one way to put it is that values without valuers are pointless. I do not mean that without valuers nothing can be of value. The idea is that the point of values is realized when it is possible to appreciate them, and when it is possible to relate to objects of value in ways appropriate to their value. Absent that possibility, the objects may exist, and they may be of value, but there is not much point to that.

Think of something of value. Not only is the appropriate response to it to respect it and to engage with it in virtue of that value, but, absent this response, its value is somehow unrealized. It remains unfulfilled. The goodness of a good fruit is unrealized if it is not enjoyed in the eating.[13] The same sense of lack of fulfilment applies to a novel destined never to be read, a painting never to be seen, and so on. Not all good things can be thought of in that way. The thought does not quite work for my wonderful friendship with John, which is destined never to come about. There is no similar sense of waste[14] here, or of something missing its fulfilment.[15] In such cases the thing of value does not yet exist. Only things of value that exist can remain unfulfilled. Nothing is unfulfilled simply because something of value could exist and does not.

That the value of objects of value remains unfulfilled, if not valued, is explained and further supported by a familiar fact. That an object has value can have an impact on how things are in the world only through being recognized. The normal and appropriate way in which the value of things influences matters in the world is by being appreciated—that is, respected and engaged with because they are realized to be of value. Sometimes the influence is different: realizing the value of something, some may wish to make sure that others do

[13] I refer to the fruit's intrinsic value as a source of pleasure. The same point can be made of its instrumental value as a source of nourishment.

[14] The notion of waste imports more than just that a good was unrealized, that its value remained unfulfilled. It suggests inappropriate conduct, letting the good remain unrealized in circumstances where this should not have happened. I do not mean to imply that this is generally true of cases where the good is not realized.

[15] If I or John never have friends at all it may be that we are unfulfilled, that our lives are lacking. But that is simply because our lives (or we) would be better if we had friends. The point I am making in the text above is different, though reciprocal. It concerns not the good (or well-being) of valuers, but the goodness of objects with value.

not have access to it, or they may destroy it or abuse it, or act in a variety of other ways. But all these cases confirm the general thought—namely, that the value of things is inert, with no influence except through being recognized.

Values depend on valuers for their realization, for the value of objects with value is fulfilled only through being appreciated, and is, rhetorically speaking, wasted if not appreciated. That explains the view that there is no point to the value of things of value without there being valuers to appreciate them, and it lends it considerable support. The view I have started defending is now but a short step away.

My claim was not only that the value of particular objects is pointless without valuers, but that the existence of values themselves is pointless without valuers. The thought is now fairly clear: what point can there be in the existence of values if there is no point in their instantiation in objects of value? If this is indeed a rhetorical question my case is made.

One final consideration may be added here. It is constitutive of values that they can be appreciated, and engaged with by valuers. This is plain with cultural values, by which I mean the values of products of cultural activities. It is a criticism of, say, a novel, that it cannot be understood. If true, it is a criticism of serial music that people cannot appreciate it, and engage with it. This consideration is less obvious with regard to other values, such as the beauty of waterfalls. But it is not surprising, nor accidental, that they are all capable of being appreciated by people. None of this amounts to a conclusive argument for the pointlessness of values without valuers. But it all supports that conclusion.

The dependence of values on valuers does not by any means prove the social dependence thesis. One reaction to the argument so far is to separate access to values from their existence. The ability to appreciate and to engage with many values presupposes familiarity with a culture. Typically appreciating them and engaging with them will require possession of appropriate concepts, and concepts are, if you like, cultural products. We have to admit, one would argue, that the existence of sublime mountains is independent of social practice, as is their beauty (unless it is the product of land cultivation, pollution, and the like). But appreciation of their beauty requires certain concepts, and certain sensitivities, which are socially dependent. On this view, the social dependence thesis has the wrong target. We should be concerned not with conditions for the existence of value, but with conditions of access to value.

This conclusion is borne out by the fact that the dependence of value on valuers must be expressed in terms of the pointlessness of values without valuers, rather than anything to do with their existence.

Temporal Elements in our Value Concepts

Yet there may be a case for going further than the relatively uncontroversial social dependence of access. The social dependence of (some kinds of) values appears to be enshrined in the structure of much evaluative thought. It is easiest to illustrate with regard to values that are subject to the special dependence thesis—that is, those that exist only if there is or has been a social practice sustaining them. Here are some examples. It is difficult to deny that opera (the art form) is a historical product that came into being during an identifiable period of time, and did not exist before that. Its creation and continued existence are made possible by the existence (at one time or another) of fairly complex social practices. The same goes for states, and for intimate friendships (for example, of the kind associated, though not exclusively, with some ideals of marriage), and in general for all art forms, and for all kinds of political structures, and social relations.[16] It

---

[16] Of these the temptation to deny dependence on social practices may be greatest with regard to intimate friendship. All one needs for that, some will say, is to have the appropriate emotion towards the other, and to be willing to act accordingly (when the emotion and willingness are reciprocated). But both the emotion, and the actions appropriate to it, are socially determined, and cannot be otherwise. I have argued for this view in *The Morality of Freedom* (Oxford: Oxford University Press, 1986), 308–13.

is therefore also natural to think that *the excellence* of operas, or excellence in directing or conducting operas, and so on, or the *excellence* of the law qua law, say the virtue of the rule of law, or of possessing legitimate authority as the law claims to do, and the *excellence* of a close friendship, as well as of virtue as a close friend, depend on the very same social practices on which the existence of opera, intimate friendships, or the law depends.

The thought that the excellences specific to opera and those specific to intimate friendship, or the state, depend on the social practices that sustain them, and that they depend on them in the same way and to the same degree that the existence of the opera, intimate friendship, and the state does, is reinforced by various commonsensical observations. Could it be that the excellence of Jewish humour existed before the Jewish people? Does it make sense to think of the transformation of the string quartet by Haydn as a discovery of a form of excellence that no one noticed before?

A further thought reinforces this conclusion. The very idea of opera, friendship, or the state is a normative idea in that we understand the concept of an opera or of friendship or of the state in part by understanding what a good opera is like, or a good, or successful friendship, or a good state. When we think of the state, as a creature of law, then the fact that the state claims supreme and comprehensive authority is part of what makes a social institution into a state.[17] The concept of the state is (among much else) the concept of a political organization claiming supreme authority. It is, therefore, the concept of a political organization that is good only if it has the authority it

---

[17] The thesis that the state is constituted by a legal order was forcefully advanced by Hans Kelsen; see his *A General Theory of State and Law* (Cambridge, Mass.: Harvard University Press, 1946). John Finnis has argued the case for the normative character of the concept of the law in his *Natural Law and Natural Rights* (Oxford: Oxford University Press, 1980), ch. 1. In *Practical Reason and Norms* (1975; 2nd edn., Oxford: Oxford University Press, 1999), ch. 5, I argued that the law is a normative system claiming authority that is both comprehensive and supreme.

claims. Its specific form of excellence determines the nature of the state.[18]

Opera, friendship, and other art forms and social forms are more fluid. But they too are to be understood, in part, by their specific virtues. Some art forms are rigid, and rigidly defined, as are Byzantine icons. Most are fluid, and their concept allows for a variety of forms, for realization in different traditions, and in different manners. Quite commonly it also allows for the continuous transformation of the genre. Even so, mastering the concept of any specific art form requires an understanding of normative standards specific to it. Opera, to give but one example, is nothing if not an art form where success depends on success in integrating words and music, such that the meaning of the work, or of parts of it, is enriched by the interrelation of word and music. This, of course, leaves vast spaces for further specification, articulation, and dispute. Not least it leaves unspecified the way in which music and words have to be related. But it is not empty: it imposes constraints on success in opera, and through this on the concept of opera.

The tendency of some disputes about the quality of art works to turn into doubts whether they are art at all manifests both the dependence of the concept of art and of different art genres on normative standards, and the fluidity of those standards, which makes it possible for artists to challenge some of them at any given time by defying them in practice. The same is true of the state, or of friendship: some friendships are so bad that they are no friendships at all.

---

[18] The claim made here that a normative standard, and a form of excellence, are part of the concept of the state does not entail that it is part of the necessary conditions for something being a state that it meets those standards. To be a state it needs to claim legitimate comprehensive authority, not to have it. However, as I point out below, at least some concepts allow for something like that. Of some kinds it is the case that objects can belong to them by degrees: this is more of a *K* than that, we can say. It is more of a holiday than the one we had last year, etc. In such cases the excellence of the kind commonly contributes to the determination of degrees of membership. And commonly there is a vague boundary between being a very bad member of the kind and not being a member at all.

If forms of art, and forms of social relations and of political organization, are constituted in part by standards for their success, then the thought that the creation of these art forms and of these political organizations is also the creation or emergence of these forms of excellence, while still obscure, seems almost compelling. As art forms, social relations and political structures are created by social practices—or, at any rate, as their existence depends on such practices—so must their distinctive virtues and forms of excellence depend on social practices that create and sustain them. In these cases, it would seem that not only access to these values, but the values themselves, arise with the social forms that make their instantiation possible. Similar arguments can show, the suggestion is, that the same is true of many other values

LIMITS OF THE SPECIAL THESIS

So far I have tried to describe and motivate the social dependence thesis, and in particular the special thesis. It is time to say something about its scope, and limitations.

The special dependence thesis seems to apply primarily to what we may call cultural values, meaning those values instantiation of which generally depends on people who have the concept of the value, or of some fairly closely related value, acting for the reason that their action or its consequences will instantiate it, or make its instantiation more likely. In plain English, these are values people need to know at least something about and to pursue in order for there to be objects with those values. They need to engage in relations with the idea that they want to be good friends, make good law in order to make good law, and so on. The excellences of the various forms of artistic activity and creativity, the values associated with the various leisure pursuits, the goods of various forms of social institutions, roles, and activities relating to them, and of various personal relations are all instances of cultural values. The special dependence thesis applies to them because sustaining practices are a necessary condition for it to be possible for these values to be instantiated, and the possibility of instantiation is a condition for the existence of values.

Four important classes of values are not subject to the special thesis. They are values the possibility of whose instantiation does not depend on a sustaining practice.

1. Pure sensual and perceptual pleasure. Sensual and perceptual pleasures are at the root of many cultural pleasures, but their pure form—the value of the pleasure of some sensations or perceptions—is not subject to the special thesis.

2. Aesthetic values of natural phenomena, such as the beauty of sunsets. As was noted before, access to them is culturally dependent, but their existence is not.

3. Many, though not all, enabling and facilitating values. These are values whose good is in making possible or facilitating the instantiation of other values. Take, for example, freedom, understood as the value of being in a condition in which one is free to act. People can be free without anyone realizing that they are free. No sustaining practice is necessary to make it possible for people to be free. I call freedom an enabling value for its point is to enable people to have a life—that is, to act pursuing various valuable objectives of their choice.

Many moral values are of this kind, though some are more complex in nature. For example, justice is an enabling value, in that denial of justice denies people the enjoyment or pursuit of valuable options or conditions, but it can also be an element of the value of relationships, in that treating the other unjustly is inconsistent with them. Those relationships are subject to the special thesis, but justice as a condition in which one is not treated unjustly is not.[19]

4. The value of people, and of other valuers who are valuable in themselves. That is, the identification of who has value in him or her self does not depend on sustaining practices.

[19] According to many views, freedom too is not merely an enabling value but a component of other values as well.

Moral values, and the virtues, rights, and duties that depend on them, often belong to the last two categories, and are thus not directly subject to the special thesis. They are, however, at least partially dependent on social practices indirectly. This is most obvious in the case of enabling values: their point is to enable the pursuit and realization of others, and, to the extent that the others are socially dependent, so are they, at least in their point and purpose.

A similar point applies to the value of people or of valuers generally. The whole point of being a valuer is that one can appreciate and respect values, and, to the extent that they are socially dependent, there is no point to being a valuer, unless there are sustaining practices making possible the existence of values.

Does that mean that values of these two categories are subject to the general thesis, at least in part—that is, at least to the extent that they depend for their point on values that are subject to the special thesis? To answer this question we need to disambiguate the general thesis. As phrased, the special thesis is about the existence of some values. The general thesis merely refers to values 'depending' on others. Do they so depend for their existence or for their point? I think that for the purpose of providing a general account of values the more significant thesis is the one that focuses on the fact that (with the exception of pure sensual pleasures, and the aesthetic values of natural objects[20]) all values depend for their point on the existence of values that are subject to the special thesis.[21]

In discussing the dependence of values on valuers I noted the case for a thesis that there is no point to values without a socially dependent access to them. In many ways, that is a more attractive thesis, for there is some awkwardness in thinking of values as existing at all. For reasons I went on to explain, it seemed to me that cultural values are conceived in ways that presuppose that they have temporal existence. They are subject to the special thesis. There is less reason to

[20] And access to those largely depends on social practices.

[21] Which is not to deny that there are some values whose existence depends on the existence of others, and that singling them out may be relevant for some purposes.

attribute temporal existence to the values that are not subject to it. We think of them as atemporal, or as eternal. What matters, however, is that they have a point only under certain circumstances. For most values their point depends on it being possible to recognize them and engage with them. They are idle and serve no purpose if this is impossible. In this sense the value of valuers depends on other values, for what is special about valuers qua valuers is their ability to engage with values. The point of enabling values is that they enable people to engage with other values. They depend for their point on there being such other values. In these ways values of these categories are partially subject to the (general) social thesis.

They are only partially subject to it, for not all other values are subject to the special thesis, and therefore the values depending on it indirectly are not entirely dependent on it. But the values that can give a meaning and a purpose to life are socially dependent. The purely sensual and perceptual pleasures are momentary pleasures; only when they are integrated within cultural values and become constituent parts of them can they become an important part of people's lives, only then can they give meaning to people's lives, and the same is true of enjoyment of the beauty of nature. Moreover, the same is true of moral requirements and virtues that are not also parts of social relations or of institutional involvement. Being a teacher, or a doctor, or even a philosopher can contribute significantly to a meaningful life. But being a non-murderer, or a non-rapist, or a person who simply gives away to others everything he has (having acquired it like manna from heaven), is not something that can give meaning to life. In sum: the life-building values are socially dependent, directly or indirectly.

In this lecture I have tried to delineate some of the outlines of and motivation for a view of the social dependence of values, which is free from relativism. In the lecture that follows I hope that some of its merits will emerge through a discussion of its relations to value pluralism, to interpretation, and to evaluative change.

Implications

The Implications of Value Pluralism

SPECIFIC AND GENERAL VALUES

Evaluative explanations travel up and down in levels of generality. Sometimes we explain the nature of relatively general values by the way they generalize aspects of more specific ones. We explain the nature of relatively specific values by the way they combine, thus providing for the realization of different, more general ones. For example, we can explain the value of friendship—which is a fairly general value standing for whatever is of value in one-on-one human relationships of one kind or another, which are relatively stable, and at least not totally instrumental in character—by reference to the more specific, to the value of various specific types of relationships. Thus, the value of friendship in general is explained by reference to the relatively distinct values of intimate friendships, of work friendships, of friendships based on common interests, and so on. On the other hand, we can explain the value of tragedies by reference to more general literary, performance, and cognitive values that they characteristically combine.

The more general the values the less appealing appears the thesis of their social dependence. The more specific the values the more appealing it appears, but at the same time the more prone we are to doubt whether these relatively specific values are really distinct values. These doubts are easily explained. Let me start with a quick word about more general values, like beauty, social harmony, love. We doubt whether there are practices sustaining such values, for their very generality challenges our common expectations of what practices are like. They are, we think, patterns of conduct performing and approving of the performance of, and disapproving of failure to perform, actions of a rather specific type in fairly specific circumstances. Things like the practice of annually giving 10 per cent of one's earnings to charity.[1] We do not think of people's behaviour towards issues involving beauty as a practice, for there is no specific action-type, performance or approval of which can constitute the practice of beauty, so to speak.

Our appreciation of beauty can be manifested by almost any conceivable action under some circumstances or other. In large part, the practices sustaining more general values are those that sustain relatively specific values that instantiate these general values (among others). Of course, the general value can be instantiated in new ways, not yet known, as well. Its scope is not exhausted by the scope of its sustaining practices. That the existing practices sustaining specific values through which a more general one is sustained do not address all possible applications of the general value does not detract from the practice counting as sustaining that value, though it may show that people have not recognized, or not recognized adequately, the general value that the practices support.

Turning to more specific values, the doubts change. Here we tend to accept that there are sustaining social practices, but we may doubt whether there are distinct values that they sustain. Is there any sense, one may ask, in regarding the psychological thriller as embodying a distinct form of excellence, and therefore a distinct value, different from that which is embodied in romantic comedies, for example? Is it not the case that both psychological thrillers and romantic comedies are good or bad to the extent that they succeed or fail in embodying general values, such as being entertaining, insightful, beautiful to watch, and so on?

---

[1] This is particularly clear if one conceives of a practice along the line of H. L. A. Hart's explanation of social rules in *The Concept of Law* (1961; 2nd edn., Oxford: Oxford University Press, 1994).

I have to admit that when referring to values *as values,* which mercifully we do not do too often, we have in mind fairly general values like freedom, beauty, dignity, or happiness. However, it is impossible to understand the value of everything that has some value as merely an instantiation of one or more of these general values. What is good about romantic comedies is not just that they are optimistic, generous about people, well plotted, and so on (and not even all of these are very abstract values) but also the special way in which they combine these qualities, which may be all that distinguishes some romantic comedies from some domestic dramas, which otherwise may display the same values. Many specific values, specific forms of excellence, have this structure: objects belonging to the relevant kind instantiate that relatively specific value if they combine various other values in a particular way. They are distinct values because of the special mix of values they are. When talking of genre- or of kind-constituting values I will have such values in mind.

The concept of a genre or a kind of value combines two features: it defines which objects belong to it, and in doing so it determines that the value of the object is to be assessed (*inter alia*) by its relations to the defining standards of the genre.

Each literary or artistic genre or sub-genre is defined by a standard, more or less loosely determined, setting the criteria for success in the genre, the criteria for being a good instance of the genre. The standard of excellence set by each genre is identified not only by the general values that go to make it, but by their mix, the nature of their 'ideal' combination. This is not to deny that there usually are also other criteria definitive of genres, and other criteria for being an instance of a genre (like ending with a wedding).[2]

---

[2] Is it not necessary that there are additional criteria for belonging to a genre? Not so. Some genres may be such that any item belongs to them if, were it to belong to them and be judged by their standard of excellence it would be ranked higher than if it were to belong to and be judged by the standard of any alternative genre. In such cases the value specific for the genre provides the specific content for the criterion of being an instance of the genre. But this is a special case, and most genres have additional criteria of membership though relative success may be one of the criteria.

Some may object to the suggestion that all appreciation in literature, music, and the visual arts is genre dependent. In any case, a serious question arises whether these conclusions can be generalized
outside the arts, even assuming that I am right about them.

Do we still rely on genre in the evaluation of works of literature,
art, or music? Have not composers abandoned the categories of
symphony, concerto, and so on? Have not the boundaries of novel,
novella, short story been eroded? Has not the very distinction
between a narrative of fact and fiction been successfully challenged?
In any case, can one hope to detect genre-based thinking outside the
understanding and appraisal of literature and the arts?

These doubts are exaggerated. It is true that writers and composers have broken loose from the hold of what we may call traditional genres. It is also true that the process was not one of replacing
old genres with new ones, at least not if genres are understood as
imposing the same stringent rules that the old ones obeyed.[3] We are
in a period of greater fluidity and flexibility. But that does not mean
that evaluative thought in general is not genre based. That notion
allows for all these flexibilities.

I have contributed to the misunderstanding on which the objection is based, by using the term 'genre', alluding to formal musical
and literary genres. It seemed helpful to start with an analogy to a
familiar application of what I call genre-based or kind-based
thought—namely, its application to works that fall squarely within
the boundaries of a specific and fairly well-defined genre, such as a
Shakespearian sonnet, or a sonata form, or a portrait painting. It is
time to abandon the analogy, and allow for the full flexibility and
complexity of the idea.

Its gist is in the two-stage process of evaluation: we judge the
value of objects by reference to their value or success as members of
kinds of goods. Is this a good apple, we ask? Or, did you have a good
holiday? Was it a good party? Was it a good lecture? Is he a good

---

[3] The failure of 12-tone technique to take hold is an instructive example.

father? In all these cases the noun ('apple', 'party', and so on) does more than help in identifying the object, event, or act to be judged. It identifies the way it is to be judged.[4] This object has some value because it is a good apple, it was time well spent because it was a good party, that is because the event was good as a party, and so on. The habit of evaluating by kinds is so instinctive that we may fail to notice it. It is odd to say: 'The lecture was good because it was a good lecture.' But that is how it is. The lecturer's activity is of value because it was successful as a lecture. The two-stage procedure is essential to the idea of what I call a genre-based evaluation, and these examples illustrate how pervasive is its application outside the arts.

Perhaps paradoxically, membership of a genre is not, however, essential to the process. Capote's *In Cold Blood*, we may say, is neither a novel nor a documentary, but creates a new terrain somewhere in between. We then appreciate it in relation to the standards of excellence both of reportage and of novels, judging whether it deviates arbitrarily or sensibly, whether the deviation contributes to its merit, or detracts from it. Genre-dependent evaluation is marked by the fact that objects are evaluated by reference to kinds, to genres. But there are different relations they can bear to the genre. Straightforward membership or exemplification of the kind is only one of them. Two elements determine how items can be evaluated. First is the definition of the kinds of goods to which they relate, which includes the constitutive standards of excellence for each kind.

[4] Evaluation with reference to kinds has, of course, been often discussed by philosophers. For example, J. Urmson ('On Grading', *Mind*, 59 (1950), 145–69, and *The Emotive Theory of Ethics* (London: Hutchinson, 1968)) used it to introduce an element of objectivity into evaluative thought at a time when emotivism seemed to reign, Philippa Foot relied on it to establish the relativity of evaluations to points of view, as part of a rejection of universalist ethical views such as utilitarianism; see her *Virtues and Vices* (Oxford: Blackwell, 1978). See also G. H. von Wright, *The Varieties of Goodness* (London: Routledge & Kegan Paul, 1963), for a more complex view. The view explained here differs from theirs by (1) claiming that objects can relate to kinds in a variety of ways, of which exemplification is only one; (2) allowing for detachment—that is, for transition from good of a kind to good, while retaining the umbilical cord to one's kind as the ground for the detached judgement.

Second are the ways the item relates to the kinds. It may fall square-ly within them. Or it may, for example, relate to them ironically, or iconoclastically, or as a source of allusions imported into something that essentially belongs to another kind, to create ambiguities, so that the item under discussion enjoys a duck/rabbit effect: you see it belonging to one kind one moment and to another kind the next moment.

Both kinds and ways of relating to them are sustained by social practices, and are defined in part by standards of excellence specific to them. Some periods, formal ones, tend to hold kinds rigid, allowing little change, and tend to restrict the ways objects can relate to a kind to a few well-defined patterns. Others, and our time is one of those, allow, even encourage, great fluidity and openness to change in their recognized kinds, and a fluid, rich variety of ways in which items can relate to them.[5] But these ways of relating to evaluative kinds or genres are themselves fixed by criteria that explain what they are and how they work, and therefore how objects or events that exploit them are to be assessed.

I do not claim that all objects of evaluation are instances of good or bad kinds, nor that all objects that are either good or bad are instances of such kinds, nor that those that are instances of kinds of goods or of bads are evaluated exclusively as instances of the kind. Saying this is merely to repeat the obvious. A novel may be a superb novel and yet immoral for advocating wanton violence, and so on.[6] I dwelt on genre- or kind-based values because they illustrate clearly the possi-bility of social dependence without relativism.

---

[5] Compare the example of fashion, and the different ways of relating to it, dis-cussed in my book *Engaging Reason* (Oxford: Oxford University Press, 2000), 147–8.

[6] There is, of course, the familiar claim that being immoral makes the novel bad as a novel. I think that the verdict on this one is: it depends. Sometimes it does, sometimes it does not. It depends on whether the objectionable aspect is well integrated in the work, or is relatively isolated within it.

DIVERSITY WITHOUT RELATIVISM: THE ROLE OF GENRE

Value pluralism has become a fairly familiar doctrine in recent times. Its core is the affirmation (a) that there are many distinct values— that is, values that are not merely different manifestations of one supreme value—and (b) that there are incompatible values, incompatible in that they cannot all be realized in the life of a single individual, nor, when we consider values that can be instantiated by societies, can they be realized by a single society. If a person or a society has some of them, they are necessarily deficient in others. It is commonly understood to mean that the values that we fail to realize, or some of them, are as important as the values that we can realize, and that this is generally true both for individuals and for societies. So that, even if individuals and societies are as good as they can be, they are not perfect, nor can they be ranked according to the kind of value they exemplify.[7]

In spirit,[8] as I see it, value pluralism is committed to the view that there are many incompatible and yet decent and worthwhile routes through life, and that they are as available to people in other civilizations, and were as available to people in other generations, as they are to us. Such views, which underlie the writings of Isaiah Berlin and of Michael Walzer, to name but two, reject the hubris of the moderns who believe that our ways are superior to those of all other human civilizations. I mention this here because the spirit of value pluralism courts contradiction.

[7] Various alternative understandings of pluralism abound, from mere satisfaction of the first condition above through to forms of pluralism that include hostility or competitiveness between supporters of different values. My characterization of pluralism here is stronger than mere satisfaction of the first condition, for my interest is in those aspects of pluralism that force people to choose among values, force them to give up on some in order to pursue others (at all or to a higher degree).

[8] That is, this feature is not entailed by the two characteristics by which I defined value pluralism, but is assumed by many of its supporters, and is an essential part of their general view of value.

Values are contradictory when one yields the conclusion that something is good, and the other the conclusion that that very thing is, in virtue of the same properties, without value, or even bad. The spirit of pluralism in affirming the value of different cultures, their practices and ideals, runs the risk of affirming contradictory values. Can one affirm value diversity without contradiction? Can one do so without abandoning our critical ability to condemn evaluative beliefs, regardless of their popularity, and regardless of their rootedness in some culture or other?

Relativism handles apparent contradictions by confining the validity of values to particular times and places, or to particular perspectives. In doing that, however, social relativism runs the risk of having to recognize the validity of any value that is supported by the practices of a society, so long as no contradiction is involved in the recognition. It has too few resources for criticizing the evaluative beliefs of other societies.[9] The social dependence thesis avoids this pitfall. Unlike social relativism, it does not hold that social practices limit the application or validity of values. The test of whether something is valuable or not is in argument, using the full range of concepts, information, and rules of inference at our disposal. So far as the soundness of claims of value are concerned, the social dependence of value is neither here nor there. It makes no difference.[10]

Can, one may therefore wonder, the social dependence thesis accommodate the spirit of pluralism?[11] Is it not condemned to judge most apparently contradictory values to be really contradictory? I think that the spirit of pluralism can be accommodated within the framework of the social dependence thesis partly

[9] Not that every relativist will acknowledge that as a difficulty. It is a reform of our ways of thinking about values that relativists are committed to.

[10] At least in general it makes no difference. I do not mean to deny the possibility of some views about specific values that are inconsistent with the social dependence thesis, and therefore refuted by it.

[11] The thought of the possibility of accommodation is meant to leave it open whether in any particular case an apparent contradiction is a real contradiction.

because it can embrace local relativism, as can any other view, but mainly because evaluative thought is so heavily genre or kind dependent.

We are intuitively familiar with the phenomenon in our understanding of literature, music, films, art and architecture, and others. But the same applies to values in other domains. We can admire a building, and judge it to be an excellent building for its flights of fancy, and for its inventiveness. We can admire another for its spare minimalism and rigorous adherence to a simple classical language. We judge both to be excellent. Do we contradict ourselves? Not necessarily, for each displays the virtues of a different architectural genre—let us say, romantic and classical.[12]

The vital point is that judgements of merit (and of demerit) proceed in such cases in the two steps discussed earlier. We identify the work as an instance of one genre, and judge it by the standards of that genre. If it is a good instance of its genre, then it is a good work absolutely, not only good of its kind. Judgements of works as being good of their kind do not yield the appearance of contradiction. No suspicion of contradiction is aroused by judging one church to be an outstanding Byzantine church, and another to be a very good Decorated Gothic church, even though conflicting standards are applied in the judgements—that is, even though features that make one good (as a Byzantine church) would make the other bad (as a Decorated Gothic church). The appearance of contradiction arises when we generalize from genre-bound judgements to unrestricted evaluative judgements, finding both of them good for apparently contradictory reasons. This may lead one to endorse an evaluative account we may call genre relativism, permitting genre-relative evaluations, but holding that unrestricted evaluations are meaningless. However, we regularly indulge in such unrestricted evaluations,

---

[12] To simplify the presentation I will revert to referring only to simple instantiation of one kind in the examples, leaving out the complex relationships objects can have to kinds, as explained above.

and there is in fact nothing wrong with them.[13] The point to bear in mind is that unrestricted judgements are based on genre-related standards. The work is good because it is good by the standards of its genre.[14] While the verdict (good, bad, or mediocre) is unrestricted, its ground is always relative to a particular genre. Thus contradiction is avoided.

The same ways of resolving apparent contradictions apply outside the arts. One system of criminal justice is good to the extent that it is a good adversarial system; another is good to the extent that it is a good prosecutorial system. Excellence in being an adversarial system is, in part, in features, absence of which is among the conditions of excellence in being a prosecutorial system of justice. Nevertheless, the two systems may be no worse than each other, each being good through being a good instance of a different, and conflicting, kind.

Are not the examples I give simple cases of local relativism? Local relativities, of the 'in Rome do as the Romans do' kind, are obviously important in facilitating the spirit of pluralism. Manifestations or applications of local relativism are usually taken to be, and some are, independent of genre- or kind-based considerations. They rely on nothing more than the fact that, to apply to a particular set of circumstances, a relatively general value has to be realized in a way that will not be suitable for other circumstances.

We are used to appealing to such considerations to explain why different, incompatible forms of marriage, and of other social rela-

[13]   This does not mean, of course, that it is always possible to rank works belonging to different genres by their degree of excellence. Quite often such works are of incommensurate value. The points made in the text apply primarily to non-comparative, but unrestricted judgements of value, though they signify that one necessary precondition of comparative judgements obtains.

[14]   Among the many questions this view brings to mind: how is membership of genre determined? Criteria of membership of a genre are themselves genre determined, and may differ from genre to genre. They are, in other words, determined by the sustaining practices of the genre. Since the standards of each genre determine membership in it, multiple memberships are possible, and not all that rare. This may lead to diverse judgements, as the work may be good in one genre and not so good, or even bad, in another, leading to indeterminacy regarding its unrestricted standing.

tions, were valuable at different times. We rarely test the hypothesis that this was made necessary by differing circumstances, and I suspect that often no such justification of diversity is available. The factual considerations involved are too complex to be known. True, in many such cases the local forms of relationships are suitable to local circumstances simply because they took root there, and people have become used to them, to living by them. This is a good reason for not disturbing them if they are valuable. But they are not valuable because they are the only way to implement some general value. Rather they are one of several possible valuable but incompatible arrangements to have. The argument for their value depends on a genre- or kind-based argument to defend their value against charges of contradiction because of their incompatibility with other valuable arrangements.[15]

Many of the diversities in forms of personal relations, as well as the case of adversarial versus prosecutorial systems of criminal justice,[16] and many others, can be reconciled only via a local relativism that, to explain away apparent contradictions, relies on, and presupposes, genre- or kind-based evaluations.

Change and Understanding

UNDERSTANDING AND VALUE

To the extent that it is possible to distinguish them, my emphasis so far has been on ontological questions, on the existence of values. It is

[15] I have discussed the application of this form of local relativism as applied to constitutions in 'On the Authority and Interpretation of Constitutions: Some Preliminaries', in Larry Alexander (ed.), *Constitutionalism* (New York: Cambridge University Press, 1998).

[16] Needless to say there can be shortcomings in each system that have to be remedied and that sometimes can be remedied by borrowing elements from another system, even one that is based on incompatible principles. Respect for valuable diversity is not to be confused with conservative opposition to sensible reform.

time to shift to questions of understanding of values, remembering all along that the two cannot be entirely separated.

Understanding, rather than knowledge, is the term that comes to mind when thinking of evaluative judgements. Judgement, rather than mere knowledge, is what the practically wise person possesses. Why? What is the difference? It is a matter of degree, with understanding and judgement involving typically, first, knowledge in depth, and, second, and as a result, knowledge much of which is implicit. Understanding is knowledge in depth. It is connected knowledge in two respects. First, knowledge of what is understood is rich enough to place its object in its context, to relate it to its location, and its neighbourhood, literally and metaphorically. Second, knowledge of what is understood is also connected to one's imagination, emotions, feelings, and intentions. What one understands one can imagine, empathize with, feel for, and be disposed to act appropriately towards. Understanding tends to involve a good deal of implicit knowledge precisely because it is connected knowledge. Its richness exceeds our powers of articulation.

Understanding is displayed, and put to use, through good judgement. To illustrate the point think of a simple example of good judgement. Jane, we may say, is a good judge of wines. Ask her which wine to serve with the meal. John, by way of contrast, has perfect knowledge of the bus timetable. You should ask him which bus to take, but it would be odd to think of him as being a good judge of bus journeys, or as having a good judgement of bus journeys, in the way that Jane is clearly a good judge of wine because of her excellent judgement regarding wines. The difference is that John's views, perfect though they are, are based on one kind of consideration, whereas Jane is judging the bearing of a multitude of factors on the choice of wine. Moreover, the ways the different factors bear on each other, and on the ultimate choice, defy comprehensive articulation. If she is articulate and reflective (and to possess good judgement she need be neither), she may be able to explain every aspect of every one of her decisions, but she cannot describe exhaustively all aspects of her decisions, let alone provide a general detailed and contentful[17] procedure for arriving at the choices or opinions she may reach on different real and hypothetical occasions, as John can.

It is not difficult to see why values call for understanding and judgement. The connection is most evident regarding specific values. They are mixed values, constituted by standards determining ways for ideal combinations of contributing values, and criteria for various relationships that objects can have to them (simple instantiation, inversion, and so on). Their knowledge requires knowledge of the various values that combine in their mix, and of the way their presence affects the value of the object given the presence of other values. Regarding these matters whose complexity and dense texture defy complete articulation, knowledge is connected and implicit, amounting, when it is reasonably reflective and reasonably complete, to understanding, and its use, in forming opinions and in taking decisions, calls for judgement.

The case of general values may be less clear. The more general the value, the more homogeneous and simple it is likely to be. Can one not have knowledge of it without understanding, and apply it without judgement? The apparent simplicity of general values is, however, misleading. To be sure, one can have limited knowledge of them, as one can of more specific values, without understanding. One can know that freedom is the value of being allowed to act as one sees fit. Such one-liners are true so far as they go. We find them useful because we have the background knowledge that enables us to read them correctly. Relying on abstract formulations of the content of values, and *denying* that they need to be understood in context and interpreted in the light of other related values, leads to one of the most pernicious forms of fanaticism.

---

[17] It is always possible to provide thin descriptions of such procedures: you consider the impact of all relevant factors on your overriding goal, and, mindful of the need to protect other matters of concern to you, you reach a decision that will be best in the circumstances. I do not mean formal or thin descriptions like this.

As I have already mentioned, more general values are explained at least in part by the way they feed into more specific ones. The point can be illustrated in various ways, appropriate to various examples. There could be forms of friendship different, some quite radically so, from those that exist today. But one cannot pursue friendship (a relatively general value) except through the specific forms it has (this comment will be somewhat qualified when we discuss innovation and change below). Therefore, knowledge of the value of friendship is incomplete without an understanding of its specific forms, with their specific forms of excellence.

INTERPRETATION

Hopefully you found my remarks on the connectedness of knowledge about values, and its relation to understanding and judgement, persuasive. If so you may be wondering how much we can know about values.

The problem arises out of the fact that so much of our evaluative knowledge is implicit. This means that a considerable degree of disagreement is inevitable. Transmission of implicit knowledge depends on personal contacts. In mass mobile societies disagreements are liable to sprout. Disagreement about values undermines the very possibility of evaluative knowledge, at least so far as cultural values are concerned, and for the remaining time I will discuss only them.[18]

The nature of cultural values is determined in part by a standard of excellence, implicit knowledge of which is part of the conditions for possessing the value concept. The concept and the value are thus interdependent. The standard, you will remember, depends on a sustaining practice. The novel, for example, emerged as a distinct genre with its distinctive standard of excellence with the emergence of a sustaining practice. It could have been otherwise. A different value

---

[18] Much of what I will say applies, if at all, to other values as well, but the arguments that establish that will not be considered here.

might have emerged had that practice not developed, and had another one, sustaining a different standard, emerged in its place. The process is continuous: the early Victorian novel develops into the mid-Victorian novel as the standard by which novels are judged changes with changes in the underlying sustaining practices—that is, with changes in the concepts involved, or, if you like, with the emergence of new concepts referring to the modified standards by which novels come to be judged.

Disagreements about the application of the concepts, those that cannot be explained by faulty information, or other factors, mean that matter lies within the area regarding which the concept is vague. Here then is the problem: the value is determined by the standard of excellence set by the sustaining practice, and enshrined in the value concept. Where the value concept is vague, because, owing to disagreements about it, there is no common understanding of its application to some cases, what are we to think?

One temptation is to go down a radical subjectivist escape route, and deny that evaluative disagreement is anything other than a difference of taste. There is no fact about which people disagree. They just like different things. Nothing in the story so far would, however, warrant this extreme reaction. The disagreement is limited, and does not warrant denying that we know that Tolstoy is a better novelist than Mrs Gaskell, or that a fulfilling relationship can make all the difference to the quality of one's life, and many other evaluative truths. Furthermore, the nature of the disagreements we are considering tends to affirm rather than challenge the objectivity of values, and the possibility of evaluative knowledge. These disagreements are contained within a framework of shared views: that being imaginative contributes to the excellence of a novel, that being loyal contributes to the excellence of a relationship, and so on. The disagreement is about the way the elements relate, about their relative importance, and the like. It is bounded disagreement that makes sense only if the agreement makes sense, and the agreement is that, regarding these boundary matters, people are justified in their claim to knowledge. We need to find a way of dealing with the intractability of local disagreements without denying the possibility of evaluative knowledge in general.

What other options are there? The epistemic option[19] is not available. That option claims that the vagueness of evaluative concepts is due to people's ignorance of their precise nature, and hence their tendency to make mistakes in their application. In truth, regarding each case there is, according to the epistemic option, a fact of the matter: either it is or it is not an instance of the value. In cases of vagueness we are, perhaps inescapably, unaware of it. Groping in the dark, unsurprisingly we disagree. This option is not available because, given that the value-defining standard is set by the sustaining practice, if the sustaining practice is vague there is no fact of the matter ignorance of which renders our understanding of the value and the value concept incomplete. There is nothing more to be known.[20]

You may think that there is no problem here. If the disagreeing parties recognize that they are dealing with a vague case, and that because of that the question whether the value concept applies to the problem case admits of no clear answer, their disagreement will evaporate. They will both withdraw their conflicting claims and say

[19] Associated with the general theories of vagueness set out by Timothy Williamson, in *Vagueness* (London: Routledge, 1994); compare Ronald Dworkin's treatment of the vagueness of what he calls 'interpretive concepts', in *Law's Empire* (Cambridge, Mass.: Harvard University Press, 1986).

[20] In this regard, the concepts of cultural values differ from the generality of concepts whose object does not depend on them, or on other closely related concepts, for its existence. Dedicated coherentists will say that the concept is determined by a coherent idealization of the practice that resolves its vagueness. I agree that the concept cannot be gauged from a statistical headcount of people's behaviour. It is, if you like the phrase, a theoretical construct based on that behaviour. But it is not subject to a completeness requirement simply because there are not enough resources to prefer one way of completing it over the others. For my discussion of concepts, which depends on some aspects of Tyler Burge's account, see 'Two Views of the Nature of the Theory of Law. A Partial Comparison', *Legal Theory*, 4 (1998), 261–73, repr. in J. Coleman, *Hart's Postscript* (Oxford: Oxford University Press, 2001).

that there is no answer to the question. But that option is not generally available either.[21]

First, the condition cannot always be met in cases of vagueness. That is, it cannot be the case that when a concept is vague those who have it always recognize when it is vague. If it were so, the concept would not be vague. Rather it would be a concept that precisely applies to one range of objects, does not apply to a second range of objects, and the question of its application to the third range does not arise, regarding which it neither applies nor does not apply.

Regarding cultural values the problem is worse. The existence of a sustaining practice is a condition of their existence because the possibility of their instantiation requires that people understand something about their nature, and that understanding will be implicit and requires a practice to be generated, and transmitted. But the practice is not what explains why the standard of excellence is a standard of excellence. That is explained by reference to ordinary evaluative considerations. Therefore, where some people believe that the value concept applies to an object and others deny that it does, both sides appeal to evaluative considerations in justifying their views. Neither side appeals to the sustaining practice. The fact that it does not settle the issue cannot be invoked by either side. Therefore, the option of simply acknowledging that the case is a vague case and that none of the rival views is true is not always[22] available to them.

Moreover, retreat from a disputed domain is possible where there is something to retreat to. This is easy with concepts that admit of degree: he may not be quite bald only balding, or something like that. But with cultural values that option is not usually available. The conflicting views, once fleshed out, are conflicting accounts of the

---

[21] Though it is available in some cases.

[22] It is sometimes available—that is, when considerations other than appeal to the sustaining practices can be relied upon to establish the vagueness. This point will resurface below.

standard of excellence for the kind.[23] While sometimes a relatively small retreat from each of the rival accounts can resolve the difference, allowing for an undetermined terrain, this is not always so. The rival accounts may cut across each other, leaving no room for such mutual retreat.

This makes this kind of evaluative disagreement resemble cases of aspect seeing or Gestalt shifts. Think of a duck/rabbit shape. I look at it and see a duck. I look again, and, usually with some effort, I switch and see a rabbit. I still know that it is a duck as well. Both perceptions are correct. Thinking about values does not rely on direct perception in this way. But disagreements due to the underdetermination of values, and the vagueness of value concepts, bear analogy to aspect seeing.[24] In them too one can, if one tries, appreciate the force behind the other person's account of the value. Yet, that does not open the way to a partial modification of these accounts. Rather, typically one remains faithful to one's own account while acknowledging that the other's has force to it as well. Sometimes one does not. One can come to have both accounts and rely on each on different occasions.

Can the holders of rival and incompatible views both be right? In spite of the initial implausibility, and the difficulties that this view creates, I believe that that is often the situation. We are not considering all possible disagreements about value. In many disagreements at least one side is in the wrong. We are concerned only with disagreement where the sustaining practice underdetermines the issue. That is why it is tempting to say that there is no fact of the matter that can settle the dispute. Disagreements of this kind have two features: they are fairly general, and they cannot be explained away by ignorance or mistake.

Remember that the relations of concepts and of the values that depend on them and their sustaining practices are rather loose.

[23] Cf. Ronald Dworkin, *Law's Empire* (Cambridge, Mass.: Harvard University Press, 1986).

[24] See, on aspect seeing, Stephen Mulhall, *On Being in the World: Wittgenstein and Heidegger on Seeing Aspects* (London: Routledge, 1990).

Practices underdetermine the nature of the values they sustain when, owing to the relatively loose connection required, while they can rightly be claimed to support some particular standard of excellence, the claim that they support it is no better than the claim that they support another standard. When people's disagreements about the nature of a value are irresolvable they are so because they have, or can develop, ways of understanding the value that all conform with the commonly understood features of the value, what I called the boundaries of agreement, but diverge in their view of how they fit together, how they relate to each other, about their relative importance, and whether they contribute to the value in dispute for one reason or another.

People unfamiliar with the value concept would not be able to participate in the argument at all. Both diverging accounts have a good deal in common, and both present an attractive standard of excellence. Of course, one may like objects that excel by one standard better than objects that excel by the other standard. But that possibility is inherent in the approach to value I am developing: values guide action, they guide our imagination and our taste, but there are many of them and one's taste may favour some rather than others. Articulate people familiar with the value concept can give a (partial) account of it, and I will assume that they are not making mistakes. Nevertheless, their account will inevitably be vague in some ways in which the concept is not, and not vague in some ways in which the concept is. It may be as good an account as one can give and yet there will be others no worse than it, but different, and incompatible in that they cannot all be part of one account.

This is why accounts of values deserve to be regarded as interpretations of the values they are accounts of. Interpretations are explanations (or displays) of meaning that can be rivalled. That is why we feel that they are more subjective: Brendel's interpretation of Schubert's B-flat sonata is no less good than, though very different from, that of Kovasevich, and it tells us something about Brendel as well as about the sonata. An explanation of how genes determine people's eye colour is not an interpretation, not because there can be only one such explanation, but because all the explanations are compatible with each other. They tell us little about those who give them other than their ability to explain.

Interpretations are explanations where diverse incompatible explanations can be correct. This multiplicity of correct rival interpretations explains why they are so revealing of their authors.[25] But it does not show, as some suppose, that interpretations are no more than a matter of taste. Some interpretations are straightforwardly wrong; others though holding some truth are inferior to their rivals. In short, the concept of interpretation provides us with the features we wanted: it is governed by objective standards, yet it allows that the phenomena underdetermine their interpretation, and can be interpreted in various ways none worse than the others. This allows them to be revealing of the interpreters, as well as of those who prefer one interpretation to the others.

Like aspect seeing, interpretations admit both of fixity and of flexibility. That is, it takes an effort for people to see the sense of rival interpretations, and the common belief that if I am right the other must be wrong is no help in this. Even after one sees the merit of a rival interpretation, there may be only one that one feels at home with. Yet some people can be at home with various ones, and feel free to rely on them on different occasions.

We display this complexity by regarding some interpretative statements as true, or false, others as right or wrong, and others still as more or less correct, or as good interpretations, an appellation that allows for the possibility of others no less good. We need to free ourselves from the rigidity of the division of domains of thought into those that are either objective and entirely governed by the true/false dichotomy, and those that are entirely subjective and are mere matters of taste. There are many other reasons for breaking out

---

[25] Though, of course, mistakes and wrong interpretations can also be revealing of their authors.

of this straitjacket. But unless we do so we will not be able to understand our understanding of values.

INTERPRETATION AND CHANGE

One way of putting my response to doubts about evaluative knowledge that derive from the perennial nature of some kinds of evaluative disagreement is that we can know more than those who deny the possibility of evaluative knowledge suppose, and less than many of their opponents think, or that we can know something, but less than is sometimes imagined. My tendency to explain the possibility of knowledge at the expense of many knowledge claims was evident in my account of the kind- or genre-based nature of many evaluative judgements. Since many value judgements are genre based, they allow for knowledge, based on the defining standards of the genre, and avoid contradiction, since different objects that belong to different kinds can be judged by otherwise contradictory standards.

The underdetermination of value by practice, which is an inevitable consequence of the social dependence of value, confronted us with a different problem. However, my response was similar. I claimed that both sides in such disputes can be right. This time recognition of this fact requires not realization that criteria of value are kind based, but a loosening of the rigid divide between matters of knowledge and matters of taste, between the domain of truth and that of preference. The realization both of the kind dependence of value judgements and of the interpretative nature of many value judgements requires greater toleration of diversity than is common. It requires abandoning many claims to exclusive truth. But those are also required of us if we are not to make claims that the subject does not warrant.

The tendency to account for evaluative knowledge through moderating its ambition is common to important strands in contemporary philosophy. My motivation differs from that of most of these writers in that I am not concerned with reconciling evaluative knowledge with a naturalistic metaphysics, nor with the alleged problem of how evaluative beliefs can motivate.[26] This may account for some of the differences in the positions we favour.

The softening of the distinctions between knowledge and taste, truth and preference, that I am urging arises out of the social dependence of value, with the result that, at least where cultural values are concerned, the proper contours of values are vague and their existence is in a flux. This results in the centrality of interpretation in evaluative thinking. Interpretation also provides the bridge between understanding of what there is and creation of the new. The crucial point is to see how this transition can be gradual, almost unnoticed. Of course it is not always like that. We are familiar with pioneering, revolutionary social movements as well as with self-consciously revolutionary movements or individual attempts in the arts. The social dependence of values points to caution in understanding the contribution of such revolutionary innovations. History is replete with examples of revolutionary impulses leading people to abandon, as out of fashion or worse, the pursuit of familiar values, in search of some vision of the new and better. It is much rarer for those visions to come true as intended. The new forms of the good take time, and require the density of repeated actions and interactions to crystallize and take a definite shape, one that is specific enough to allow people intentionally to realize it in their life or in or through their actions. When they settle they commonly turn out to be quite a bit different from the revolutionary vision that inspired them.

Be that as it may, it is of interest to see how the familiar fact that change can be imperceptible is explained by the facts adumbrated so far. Two processes are available, and the distinction between them is often too vague to allow a clear diagnosis when one or the other occurs. First, one may like a variant on the norm, and that may catch on, and become the standard for a new norm. Second, one or another

---

[26] My response to the first issue is outlined above, in 'Dependence Without Reduction', in 'The Thesis', and to the issue of motivation in ch. 5 of *Engaging Reason* (Oxford: Oxford University Press, 2000).

of the interpretations of a value, even if it is no better than its rivals because the value is underdetermined, may gain wide acceptance and affect the practice, shifting it to a new standard. In this case the change is relatively conservative, typical of the way kinds drift over time, imperceptibly, or at least unperceived at the time. What has been underdetermined by the old kind becomes the clear standard of the new kind. The important point to make is that the social dependence of values enables us to understand better such developments, and their general availability. It enables us to reconcile the objectivity of values with their fluidity and sensitivity to social practices, to shared understanding and shared meanings. It enables us to combine holding to a fixed point of reference, which is essential to thinking of values as objective, and being able to orient ourselves by them, either by trying to realize them, or through more complex relations to them, and realizing that their fixity is temporary and fragile, which explains how change is often continuous, and no different from their further development in one way rather than another, which was equally open. None of this is explainable unless we take seriously the contingency at the heart of value.

Comments

The Dependence of Value
on Humanity

Christine M. Korsgaard

I begin with one of Raz's own examples. We admire one building for its flights of fancy and inventiveness; we admire another for 'its spare minimalism and rigorous adherence to a simple classical language' (p. 45). The values we find embodied in the two buildings seem opposed, almost contradictory. Do we contradict ourselves? Not necessarily, according to Raz, for the buildings represent two different architectural genres, the romantic and the classical: each of the buildings may be a good building of its kind.

From this apparently innocuous conclusion we can work backwards to Raz's more controversial ideas. The example helps to show that what may look at first glance like an instance of social or cultural relativism is actually just a case of social or cultural *dependence*. The values of romantic architecture depend upon a practice—namely, the practice of romantic architecture. This practice arose within a particular culture, at some particular time and place. The people who practise romantic architecture are, in some sense, trying to realize the values of romantic architecture. The qualifier 'in some sense' is needed here, as Raz reminded us in his first lecture, for the practitioners might not have been able to describe themselves in *just* that way. We can easily see this by switching to the other side of the example. The first practitioners of classical architecture could hardly have described themselves as trying to realize the values of classical architecture, since of course those values had not yet become *classical*. But the earliest classical architects were presumably doing something we could count as trying to realize the values of classical architecture: say, they were aiming at a certain symmetry or serenity or solidity that people later came to identify as classical.

But now we might wonder whether that very description under-cuts the thesis that values are socially dependent. Symmetry and serenity and solidity are not, or anyway not obviously, socially dependent attributes, and if these attributes are the values in ques-tion, then the values are not socially dependent either. Whatever we decide about that question, Raz will reply, it is not an objection, because a list of such attributes is only a kind of shorthand way of referring to the relevant values anyway. The values of classical archi-tecture are not symmetry and serenity and solidity, but rather a certain characteristic way of combining these attributes, and of real-izing them in certain building materials, and in the contours and decor of rooms and entryways. The values of classical architecture are, in short, values specific to classical architecture, so specific that all we can do is gesture at them in general terms.

And that is part of the point. The values of classical architecture are in fact *so* specific to classical architecture that they can be realized only in classical architecture. Therefore until classical architecture existed, neither did its values. That is why the values depend on the practice, and only came into being with it. But once they exist, they are not relative values. I quote Raz: 'Once a value comes into being, it bears on everything, without restriction. But its existence has social preconditions' (p. 22).

As Bernard Williams also points out, that 'bears on everything, without restriction' is slightly obscure. Once the values of classical architecture exist, they bear on everything that wants to be classical architecture, to be sure. And that is *not* a normatively toothless point, for in light of it it will be true that some buildings are badly done, whether anyone thinks so or not. The critic who does think so will be seeing something that is the case, not just exercising his taste. Or rather, to put the point in a better way, he *is* exercising his taste, but his taste is a form of intelligent perception, not just a source of raw likes and dislikes. But on what else do these values bear? They do not bear on seashells or toasters or rabbits—we do not judge these to be good or bad instances of classical architecture. Do they bear on other buildings? Once the values of classical architecture exist, it does become intelligible to ask whether buildings built later in the Western European tradition realize these values, but, as Raz's own example suggests, we do not necessarily think the worse of them if they do not. Does it also become intelligible to ask whether buildings built later in Africa, or if it so happens on Mars, realize these values? I do not find this obvious myself. And if not, one might think this is a kind of cultural relativism after all. Cultural relativism is not supposed to be the same thing as a raw individual subjectivism of taste, and that, so far, seems to be the only position that has been rejected.

But actually I do not want to pursue this sort of argument, which I can leave to Bernard Williams.[1] My interest is not in pressing Raz in the direction of cultural or social relativism, but rather in the opposite direction: towards what we might call the natural dependence of value, specifically its dependence on an old-fashioned item called human nature.

But let me first say a word more about Raz's basic idea: a value comes into being at a particular time, but once it comes into existence it bears on everything. It might seem paradoxical to say that values are the contingent products of historical events, and yet that they are eternal, which is what Raz is saying. But actually the structure here is one that we should recognize. For I think that this is true—and that most of you think it is true—of *people*, normatively considered— that is, considered as sources of reasons and bearers of rights.

Let me show you what I mean by this. Let us suppose, just for the sake of the argument, that people come into existence at birth. Of course there are controversies about this, but leave those aside for now. Compare two cases. A first woman takes drugs knowing that

---

[1] See Bernard Williams, *Ethics and the Limits of Philosophy* (Cambridge, Mass.: Harvard University Press, 1985) esp. ch. 9, for an argument that it may simply be pointless to judge one culture in terms of another culture's values.

she is pregnant, damages the fetus in some horrible way, and then decides to abort. A second woman takes drugs knowing that she is pregnant, damages the fetus in some horrible way, and brings it to term and gives birth. The first woman, in my view, may have wronged herself, may in certain circumstances have wronged the potential father, and has certainly shown a pathetic lack of reverence for life. But she has not wronged the person whom that fetus might someday have been, because there is no such person. That person, on the hypothesis that people begin to exist at birth, never came into existence. But the second woman has wronged the person whom her fetus becomes, and that person has claims against her. And this is because a person, once he does exist, is a source of reasons and rights that bear on everything, without restriction. His claims extend backwards into the past as well as forwards into the future.

The point also applies to a current debate about the preservation of the environment. Some philosophers argue that the people who will exist in the future will not have claims against us for leaving the world, as we will, overheated, polluted, biologically impoverished, and extensively paved. The people who will exist in the future will not have claims against us because they will be different individual people from the ones who would have existed if we had lived differently. Therefore we could not be wronging *them* by living as we do. I think this claim is false. Once those individual people exist, whoever they are, they will have claims against us for mucking up the world. People come into existence at a particular time, and it is utterly contingent which people happen to exist.[2] But once they exist, people are the source of objective normative claims that extend backwards into

---

[2] 'Which people' carries the odd suggestion that there is a set of potential people, some of whom come into existence: the lucky ones, so to speak. That is a thought more at home in the view I am objecting to, which identifies particular people in terms of DNA combinations. My point here is just that the existence of particular people is contingent in the same sense that the existence of particular values, according to Raz, is contingent. Raz sometimes does seem to think that there is a set of potential values, some of which come into existence.

the past and forwards into the future, and, in Raz's words, bear on everything, without restriction.

Joseph Raz thinks that values are like that. They come into being at a particular time, and it is deeply contingent which ones exist. But once they exist they exert objective normative claims that bear on everything, without restriction. This comparison between people and values is not a merely fanciful one, since, as I have tried to suggest, the two cases do have something in common: I think people are, and Raz thinks values are, the sources of normative claims.

In making these remarks I have borrowed Raz's language of 'the existence of values', which Bernard Williams in his comments objects to. So I would like to pause here and add a few words about that. One of the difficulties of philosophizing about value or perhaps especially about 'values' is that the term gets applied to a number of different kinds of items. First there are the valuable objects themselves: for instance, the operas, flowers, friendships, sunsets, and liberal governments that are serving as our examples in this discussion. Then there are the properties in virtue of which we deem these things valuable: in architecture, inventiveness, and symmetry; in friendship, intimacy, loyalty, company, and sharing; in flowers, appealing colours and shapes and scents. Third, there is the valuableness, or normative claim, that we attribute to the objects in virtue of those properties—the building is valuable in virtue of its inventiveness, the flower in virtue of its scent, say. Very abstract value terms, like beauty, may not refer to any of those things, but rather to complexes of them: we might say that a beautiful thing is an object we value in virtue of its appearance or perceptible nature, or something like that.

I think that Raz, in speaking of value, allows the term to slip around a bit among these different items, in particular between the properties in virtue of which we deem an object valuable and the value we assign to the object in virtue of those properties. The term 'excellence of', a favourite of Raz's, encourages us to slip in exactly that way. And I do not think the slip is innocuous, because I think it might be what tempts Raz to think that an object may be good in virtue of being good of its kind—a point to which I will recur shortly.

But to go back to the question of 'existence': there is obviously no difficulty about the existence of the object, and I think that any difficulty about the existence of the properties is inherited from an apparent difficulty about the existence of the third thing—the valuableness or normative claim we assign to the object in virtue of its having the properties. My own view is that talk of the existence of values at this level is just misleading shorthand for something else—namely, valuing, which is a thing that we *do*. To say that something is valuable in this sense is to say that people appropriately value it. Some people will suppose that the only way to earn the right to that 'appropriately' is to posit 'real' values 'out there in the world' that valuing, so to speak, tracks. But actually that does not follow. There is no activity—not even desiring—that you can do any way that you like. Valuing has its rules: it is something you do in virtue of a thing's properties, it is to that extent communicable to others, it trumps mere local preference, and so on. We may grant that this just moves a whole set of problems over to the activity of valuing and what its determinate limitations and demands might be. But at least it moves it over to something that unquestionably does exist—namely, the human activity of valuing—or, as I have called it elsewhere, conferring values.[3]

Let us return to the issue of pluralism. Raz notes that someone might object that he is overemphasizing the analogy between aesthetic values and values generally: aesthetic values may be relativized to genre without losing their objectivity, but this does not show that values in general may be relativized without loss of objectivity. In response to this worry Raz points out that something like genre-based thinking applies across the board. Just as a building is good or bad as a piece of classical architecture, so a lecture is good or

---

[3] Korsgaard, 'Kant's Formula of Humanity', in *Creating the Kingdom of Ends* (New York: Cambridge University Press, 1996), 106–32.

bad as a lecture, a vacation is good or bad as a vacation, and so on. There is, Raz tells us, a two-stage process embedded in evaluation: we judge a thing to be good because it is good of its kind. I quote Raz: 'It is odd to say: "The lecture was good because it was a good lecture." But that is how it is' (p. 41).

One obvious problem with this is that there are standards of excellence for very bad things: a good assassin is cool, methodical, careful, and ruthless, but we are not going to say 'the assassin is good because he is a good assassin'. Nor is it adequate merely to say that, although he may be a good assassin, we have *other* reasons to object to him. As Kant says, 'the coolness of a scoundrel makes him not only far more dangerous but also immediately more abominable in our eyes than we would have taken him to be without it'.[4] So there is the problem of the bad genre.

But there is also an issue raised by the embeddedness of the genre in another wider genre, if we take the notion this generally. To switch terms, a genre is a kind of species of a wider genus, and that may in turn be a species of a wider genus still. Aristotle thought it was the nature of the world to be divided up in this way, or perhaps we may think it is the nature of human beings to conceptualize the world in this way. This, as I am about to argue, implies that the relation between pluralism and genre-based evaluation is not as straightforward as Raz suggests.

We need not judge the romantic building to be better or worse than the classical building, or to be bad because it lacks the properties that make the classical building good. We can make room for value pluralism, because we can say that each building is good of its kind, and leave it at that. But we need not admit value pluralism merely because we have made room for it. And we may not want to admit it in all cases. Someone might think that romantic architecture is better than classical architecture, just like that. I do not mean just that he likes it

---

[4] Immanuel Kant, *Groundwork of the Metaphysics of Morals*, trans. Mary Gregor (Cambridge: Cambridge University Press, 1997), 8; in the standard Prussian Academy edition page numbers, found in the margins of most translations, p. 394.

better, but that he thinks it is better. Is that incoherent? Given the genus/species structure of the world, it should not be incoherent on Raz's account, for there is a way to make the judgement: we just back up to the wider genre or genus, and judge on the basis of values definitive of it. What is the wider genre or genus in this case? Western architecture? Decorative architecture? How about 'architecture'?

Are the values of architecture, just as such, socially dependent? No matter what society they live in, human beings must have some sort of architectural practice. Given that buildings have a general function in human life, they must meet certain universal normative standards, standards that enable them to serve those functions, and the result will be universal architectural values. And those values might *conceivably* determine that one genre is better than another.

Now we may imagine the value pluralist countering this point in the following way. Any universal architectural norms that derived from the function of buildings in human life would be instrumental norms. So the universal values of architecture, just as such, are only instrumental values: the rooms must be tall enough for people to stand up in, for instance. Now Raz asserted in the opening lines of his first lecture that instrumental values are not socially dependent, but are partly constituted by the facts. Raz's interest, in any case, is in intrinsic values. And if the argument I have just put in the pluralist's mouth were correct, then once we started judging buildings for their intrinsic values, we would have to appeal to the standards of some more specific architectural genre. All of the *intrinsic* value judgements we could make about architecture would still be socially dependent.

But I see no reason to believe that the values inherent in the practice of architecture just as such are merely instrumental. Or, to put the point in a better way, I see no reason to believe that the intrinsic/instrumental distinction is as hard and fast as all that.[5] Whatever

---

[5] That the intrinsic/instrumental distinction, using Raz's terminology for the moment, is not that hard and fast is one of the points defended in Korsgaard, 'Two Distinctions in Goodness', in *Creating the Kingdom of Ends*, 249–74. Another is that we should not use the term 'intrinsically valuable' to refer to things that are valued for

values are grounded in the genre of architecture just as such spring from the fact that buildings must be suitable for human use. And 'suitable' here can mean more than just that it is causally possible for human beings to use them. A sufficiently low ceiling might make a building literally impossible for human beings to use. But a slightly less low ceiling might be oppressive, or visually distracting, and that might be a fact that depends on our nature, rather than on cultural or social practice. I am not saying it is; the question whether a certain reaction depends on nature or culture is an empirical one, and the answer can be surprising.[6] My point is just that the genre architecture as such—or, more precisely, the genre 'building suitable for human use', *might* be the source of certain architectural values, values that could not without artificiality be categorized as instrumental. And these values would not be socially dependent. They would be dependent on human nature.

One might suppose that this sort of consideration does not apply to some of Raz's other examples—opera, for instance. Opera does not play a functional role in human life, the way buildings do. But this, to my mind, would be the same mistake again, of exaggerating how hard and fast the instrumental/intrinsic distinction is. Opera may not serve any purpose external to itself, but forms of music and storytelling seem to be common to most human societies, and activities that combine them are found in many. Opera is a genre of *something* more fundamental and broader that our nature calls for. It is

their own sakes, since that is a different idea from the idea of something's having its value within it. That point is also relevant here. The sort of value Raz ascribes to opera is intrinsic in a third sense: the standards the good opera meets spring from its intrinsic nature as opera. They are what I call 'internal standards'; and, as I have argued elsewhere, this is an important idea ('Self-Constitution in the Ethics of Plato and Kant', *Journal of Ethics*, 3 (1999), 1–29). But, as I will argue below, it does not automatically follow from the fact that something meets its internal standards that human beings have any reason to value it.

[6] The judgement that one person looks like another or that one word sounds like another feels primitive, immediate, and undeniable when you make it, as if it were just a straight sensory judgement. Yet that these judgements admit of cultural variation.

hard to give that something a name without seeming to trivialize it—as 'musical entertainment' does, for instance—but all the same there is something there.

In fact I believe there is something behind even these more fundamental and broader values; that is, something most fundamental of all. This most fundamental thing is deeply embedded in human nature, so deeply that it is difficult even to talk about, and it stands behind the whole range of our values. The Greeks called it a *logos*, Kant called it a *ground*, we might also call it a *story*, in the widest sense, as when philosophers say to each other 'you have to have some story to tell about that'. What is it? One thing does not merely follow another: it justifies it, explains it, rewards it, punishes it, it is its climax, its culmination, its fruition, or its doom. The relation between the two events or objects gives both of them meaning and intelligibility; the *direction* of the relation gives a narrative structure to what happens, hence 'story'—we tell ourselves a story. This thing is equally behind our endless delight in narratives and our thirst for scientific explanation. It is a primitive form of value, inhabiting all others, a kind of general structure of value. Whatever else it does, a good opera, a good scientific explanation, a good philosophical account, or a good passage from one room to another in a house must tell us a story. Some people think that that basic structure is given to us by the world, but as a Kantian I think that the demand for it lies in us.

But leave that aside, and come back to our more down-to-earth question about pluralism. Could the architectural values grounded in human nature, the values of architecture as such, determine a single absolutely best or right form of, say, dwelling? I do not suppose that any of us will find this *particular* possibility tempting. This is in part because among the things that human beings in fact appreciate in architecture is *variety*. And it is in part because human nature is essentially exploratory, and the generation of multiple possibilities *is* part of what our nature determines.[7] But nothing in what Raz has

---

[7] I do not know whether I have just mentioned two facts or only one.

said here rules out the theoretical possibility that our nature might determine a best or right form of house, and so no decisive case has been made for value pluralism. And this is just as well, for we might then hope that the values grounded in human nature *do* in the end determine a single absolutely best or right form of political constitution. Perhaps we can still say that it is best or right for people to live in the Kingdom of Ends. And if we can see modern constitutional forms, with their increased emphasis on equality, as moving towards that Kingdom, perhaps a little modern moral hubris will be justified after all.[8]

To prevent confusion about the point I have just made, I should say that the optimism I mean to express is about the chances of grounding a conception of the *right* in human nature that would support some particular political forms over others. Although I have challenged Raz's argument for pluralism, I do not in general find pluralism about the good implausible. On the contrary, I think that one of the most important attributes of humanity is our nearly bottomless capacity for finding sources of delight and interest in nearly *anything*, and so for conferring value on almost anything. This very fact about human nature is part of what makes it so essential that our relations to one another—both moral and political—should not be mediated by our values.[9] It is not because of our shared values that we should accord consideration to one another but because of our shared capacity for conferring value. In other words, that fact about human nature is part of what makes liberal democratic forms of the state the right ones.

---

[8] See Raz's remarks about how pluralism underlies Berlin's and Walzer's rejection of 'the hubris of the moderns who believe that our ways are superior to those of all other human civilizations' (p. 43). Raz admits that certain moral values are not socially dependent, and of course he can make an argument for the superiority of certain political forms on the basis of those. But, as I argue below, he appears to think that that is just a separate issue, and I think that misses something.

[9] See Korsgaard, 'The Reasons We Can Share', in *Creating the Kingdom of Ends*, 275–310, especially the discussion on 289–91.

Raz associates his view about the social dependence of values with a thesis that has implications for the metaphysics of intrinsically valuable objects. He says: 'The very idea of opera, friendship, or the state is a normative idea in that we understand the concept of an opera or of friendship or of the state in part by understanding what a good opera is like, or a good, or successful friendship, or a good state' (p. 31). The metaphysical implication is that opera, friendship, and the state are essentially normative entities, entities whose essence is constituted by the normative standards that govern them.

This is not to say that they have to *meet* those standards in order to be those kinds of entities, but rather that their identity is given by the fact that the standards apply to them. Actually, even 'apply to them' may be too strict in some of the aesthetic cases. Raz mentions that we live in a time of aesthetic freedom and fluidity, in which the boundaries between genres are easily crossed, and violated in other ways. In such a situation, to say that something is a member of a certain genre may mean not that it *meets* the standards of that genre and not even that it *tries to*, but only that it is possible to talk about whatever it *does* do in relation to those standards. It may be that what it does is play with the standards of a genre or comment on them or flout them deliberately. So we might count something as a novel precisely because in some identifiable way it keeps insisting that it is not a novel. It is a familiar point that many modern art forms are self-conscious and play with their own identities in this way. So we might say that things like opera, friendship, and the state are things that by their very nature want to be good opera, good friendship, or good political forms.

In a footnote in the first lecture (n. 17), Raz notes that Hans Kelsen and John Finnis thought of 'law' and 'the state' as being normative in this way. But we can go back a little further than that, for the idea that the state is in this way an essentially normative entity, only to be understood in terms of its ideal form, is the idea of Plato's *Republic*. In fact, arguably, it is *The Idea*, period. That is roughly what Plato thought.

I will come back to that point. But first, notice that Raz's point about normative identity does not apply only to intrinsically valuable cultural objects. It applies, perhaps even more obviously, to instrumentally valuable objects—that is, to useful artefacts. To know what a chair or pencil or a computer or a rocket ship is, is to know what it is supposed to do. And for these kinds of things, a good one is one that does what it is supposed to do. And to understand—not merely know, but *understand*—what such an object is, involves knowing, at least in outline, what particular normative standards to hold it to. So, just as we understand opera or friendship or the state by understanding what a good opera or a good friendship or a good state is, so we understand pencils and cars and computers by understanding what a good pencil or a good car or a good computer is, and what particular normative standards they must meet. Those who understand pencils know that they ought to have sharp points, just as those who understand classical architecture know that it ought to be spare and minimalistic, or whatever it might be.

Plato and Aristotle thought this was true of any kind of object whatever. That, as I mentioned a moment ago, is what the idea of a Platonic Form involves—that you understand any object whatever by understanding it as an attempt to meet a certain ideal form. But the view finds its clearest expression in Aristotle's *Metaphysics*. According to Aristotle, what makes an object the kind of object that it is—what gives it its identity—is what it does, or in Greek, its *ergon*: that is, its purpose, function, or characteristic activity. This is clearest in the case of artefacts. As Aristotle thinks of it, an artefact has both a form and a matter. The matter is the material, the stuff or the parts, from which the object is made. The form of the artefact is its functional arrangement or teleological construction. That is, the form is the arrangement of the matter or of the parts that enables the object to serve its function, to do whatever it does. Say, for instance, that the function of a house is to serve as a habitable shelter, and that its parts are walls, roof, chimney, insulation, and so on. Then the form of the house is that arrangement of those parts that enables it to serve as a habitable shelter—or rather, to be more precise, it is the *way* the arrangement of those parts enables it to serve as a habitable shelter.[10]

On this view, to be an object, and to have this kind of normative form—that is, to be teleologically constructed—are one and the same thing. Teleological construction is what unifies what would otherwise be, in Aristotle's wonderful phrase, a *mere heap* into a particular object of a particular kind. Teleological constuction or form is also the object of understanding: to understand a thing is to know its form. An architect is not merely someone who knows *that* the function of a house is to serve as a human habitation. We all know that. He is someone who understands *the way* building materials may be combined and put together to produce an object suitable for human habitation. So he is someone who knows the form of a house. At the same time, it is the teleological construction or form of an object that supports normative judgements about it. A house with cracks in the walls is less good at keeping the weather out, therefore less suitable for human habitation, and therefore a less good house. The ancient metaphysical thesis of the identification of the real with the good follows readily, for this kind of badness eventually shades off into literal disintegration.[11] A house with enough cracks in the walls will crumble, and cease to be a house altogether: it will disintegrate back into a *mere heap* of boards and plaster and bricks.

Aristotle extended this account of artefactual identity to living things with the aid of the view that a living thing is a thing with a special kind of form. A living thing is a thing so designed as to maintain and reproduce *itself*—that is, to maintain and reproduce its own

[10] Understanding the object is understanding *the way* the arrangement of the parts enables it to serve its function, because you could of course just see how the parts are spacially situated with respect to each other without insight as to how they work together. Then you would not know, for instance, how to make a good substitution for a missing or broken part.

[11] As Raz himself notices (in n. 18), there is vague boundary between being a very bad member of a kind and not being a member at all.

form. It has what we might call a self-maintaining form. So it is its own end; its *ergon* or function is essentially to be—and to continue being—what it is. And its organs, instincts, and natural activities are all arranged to that end. The function of a porcupine, for instance, is to be a porcupine, and to continue being one, and to produce other porcupines. Someone who really understands porcupines knows how it does that—that is, knows how the parts of a porcupine work together to keep the porcupine and its species going. Such a person, then, knows the form of a porcupine. And knowing the form of a porcupine, he is able to make the specific kind of normative judgement that applies to porcupines. He can tell when the porcupine he is considering is *healthy* or *unhealthy*, for instance.

Now let me try to make the relevance of this clear. I remind you again of the Razian thesis from which I started. Raz says: 'The very idea of opera, friendship, or the state is a normative idea in that we understand the concept of an opera or of friendship or of the state in part by understanding what a good opera is like, or a good, or successful friendship, or a good state' (p. 31). Suppose something like Plato's and Aristotle's theory of objects is true. Then it is not merely socially dependent objects like opera, friendship, and the state,[12] but any objects whatever that are, in the operative sense, normatively understood. We understand any kind of thing by understanding what a good or well-functioning thing of its kind is, and so by understanding the norms associated with it. Then we will say that Raz arrived at the idea that values and norms are socially dependent only because he happened to focus his attention on examples of socially dependent *objects*. He would otherwise have seen that value bears no special relation to socially dependent objects, for the world in so far as we can understand it is necessarily shot through with values. The fact that the norms associated with a living organic being support the normative judgements *healthy* and *unhealthy* is important here.

---

[12] Assuming for now, with Raz, that these are socially dependent objects, although I do not actually think that is true of friendship and the state.

Judgements of health are the most naturalistic of our normative judgements. No one would claim that health is a socially dependent value.

As Aristotle saw it, a living organism appears to be in the business of being what it is. That seems to be its function. Kant thought that something like this is also true of beautiful objects. They do not reproduce themselves, or act so as to keep themselves in existence, to be sure, the way a living organism does. But like living organisms, they have an overwhelming appearance of working hard at meeting normative standards that are given not by something outside themselves, but simply by their own nature. They are, as Kant says, purposive without purpose. Perhaps this is why, for Kant, biological teleology and aesthetics are two branches of the same subject: they treat two kinds of things that seem to try to meet standards given by their own nature. I note that Raz should agree with this view of aesthetic objects, since he also thinks that the function of opera, for instance, is to meet the normative standards inherent in opera. That is to say, the function of opera is to be good opera. And since opera is *defined* in terms of good opera, that in turn implies that the function of opera is to be opera. In this respect, an opera *is* like a living thing—like a porcupine, say. It is in the business of trying to be a good instance of its kind.

Perhaps, though, we will want to add that the very best aesthetic objects go beyond even this, and seem to meet standards entirely unique to their particular selves.[13] There is a terrible self-sufficiency about the most beautiful things, as if all they need is to be what they individually are. Kant, I believe, thought we encountered such things more often in nature than in art. You have got to learn to enjoy opera, and to that extent, you have to see it as the instance of a type. But take sunsets. Raz claims that the beauty of sunsets is not socially dependent, but that access to that beauty is. He thinks that appreciating sunsets is a social practice. But I think you could be dazzled by a spec-

---

[13] This is also true of the very best people, but that is a story for another day.

tacular sunset even if it is the only one you ever saw, and no one in your culture talked about such things. It might just strike you as being perfect of its kind, where its kind is given just by itself. That is what the most beautiful things are like.

Moving from the sublime to the ridiculous, I return to the healthy porcupine. I have just claimed that the criteria of a healthy porcupine are built into the very idea of a porcupine in much the same way that the criteria of an excellent opera are built into the very idea of an opera. This may make you feel that we have got derailed somewhere. Earlier I mentioned Raz's view that there is a two-stage process embedded in evaluation: we judge a thing to be good because it is good of its kind. As Raz explains, 'the habit of evaluating by kinds is so instinctive that we may fail to notice it. It is odd to say: "The lecture was good because it was a good lecture." But that is how it is' (p. 41). Maybe you do not feel very tempted to say that the porcupine is good because it is a good porcupine, or because it is a healthy porcupine. But, as I pointed out before, neither are we tempted to say that an assassin is good because she is a good assassin. The truth is that the values that are in this way internal to objects are not the end of the story. Although this is not quite Nietzsche's question, we can ask it in his words: what is the value of these values?

Someone might be tempted to say that the values realized by good assassins and healthy porcupines will not matter to you unless you care about assassins and porcupines. The question is whether you go in for such things, whether you happen to care about them. But there is no need to get subjectivistic here. The question is actually whether you have *reason* to care about the object in question. Or better, whether you *have to* care about it. My point is that the reason to care about an object is not given merely by the fact that the object realizes the values in terms of which it is defined.

You do have reason to care about the values internal to a thing, or perhaps even *have to* care about those values, when the thing is in a certain way yours. You have reason to care about your own health, for instance, because a certain physical life is yours, and your health is the excellence of that physical life. When I say that you 'have to' care about it, I mean this: you do not have to *go in* for health, the way someone might *go in* for architecture or football, in order to care about it, or to have reason to. A minimal level of concern is all but guaranteed by the fact that the body in question, the physical life in question, is yours.[14] I myself believe, although this is not the place to argue the case in detail, that there are normative standards internal to action, and that the necessity of caring about those is given by the simple fact that you have to act. The hypothetical imperative, or principle of instrumental reason, provides one example. You do not have to *go in* for instrumental reason. A minimal level of concern for your own efficacy is all but guaranteed by the fact that you have to act. Perhaps you do not thoughtfully and carefully choose the *most* effective means to your end, but you are not trying to realize an end at all unless you choose *a* means. A more controversial example, which I would also defend, is Kant's categorical imperative, the principle of autonomy. You do not have to *go in* for autonomy. A minimal level of concern for your own autonomy is all but guaranteed by the fact that your actions are, and must be, *yours*. The choice of your own law or principle is implicit in the very act of deciding what to do.

What does Raz have to say about health? I said a few minutes ago that no one would claim that health is a socially dependent value. Raz, of course, does not claim that all values are socially dependent. Instrumental values are not socially dependent. In his first lecture Raz says that health is an instrumental value; what it gets you is survival. In a footnote he adds that of course health might be valuable in other ways too. What I have already said suggests that health is not an instrumental value. Health is not a value because it gets you something—survival—but because you have already got something

---

[14] I am not saying that the fact that the physical life is yours grounds a minimal concern for it that then provides you with a reason to pursue it. I am trying to explain how the fact that the life is yours *constitutes* a reason to care about it, and explaining how the fact motivates you is part of explaining how it constitutes a reason.

of which it is the internal excellence—namely, a physical life.[15] Of course, I am not denying that there are people who try to be healthy for the sake of survival—or rather longevity.[16] People do want to be healthy in order to survive longer. But people also want to survive longer only if they will be sufficiently healthy. Raz, as we will see in a moment, thinks that the second kind of preference shows that life must contain values in order to be valuable, while on my view, it is very nearly grounded in a tautology. If health is the goodness of physical life, then the preference for living only when you are sufficiently healthy is a preference for living only when life (or at least physical life) is sufficiently good. Health is not some independently good thing that continued survival might or might not enable you to obtain or keep, something for which life provides you with an *opportunity*. I am not sure whether Raz would disagree with this or not, but he does say some things about values other than health that seem to me to be out of harmony with it, as I will explain.

Earlier I mentioned that Raz does not claim that all values are socially dependent. His theory allows for a distinction between (1) values that depend on social practices, such as those of opera; (2) values that do not depend on social practices but to which we have access only through social practices, such as the beauty of sunsets; and (3) values that are not socially dependent at all, such as instrumental values and some moral values. But Raz does want to make an

[15] In the same way, the value we set on efficacy in general is not an instrumental value. We do not adopt the hypothetical imperative, the general principle of taking the means to our ends, because adopting that principle serves some end. We could not do that, because that would be an exercise of the principle itself, and so we would already have had to adopt it. Rather, the reason we value efficacy in general is because we already have something—namely, a life constituted by action—of which its efficacy is one of the excellences. Confusion about this point is the source of much confusion in the theory of practical reason. Even Kant himself, at least in the *Groundwork*, does not get it quite right. See Korsgaard, 'The Normativity of Instrumental Reason', in Garrett Cullity and Berys Gaut (eds.), *Ethics and Practical Reason* (Oxford: Oxford University Press, 1997), 215–54.

[16] Just as there are people who try especially hard to be efficacious when the end is one that matters a lot, to follow up on the comparisons in my last footnote.

important claim about social dependence. Raz first puts forward what he calls 'the special social dependence thesis', which claims that some values depend on the existence of social practices. Then he adds what he calls a 'general social dependence thesis', which claims that 'with some exceptions, all values depend on social practices either by being subject to the special thesis or through their dependence on values that are subject to the special thesis' (p. 19).

When I first hit that phrase 'with some exceptions, all . . .', I thought it was just a curiously incautious way of saying 'most'. But it turns out there is more to it than that. Although he thinks that not all values are directly or indirectly socially dependent, Raz does think that the important values are, because 'the values that can give a meaning and a purpose to life are socially dependent' (p. 36). Raz concludes that 'the whole point of being a valuer is that one can appreciate and respect values, and, to the extent that they are social-ly dependent, there is no point to being a valuer, unless there are sustaining practices making possible the existence of values' (p. 35).

The idea that cultural values are what give life value strikes me as being wrong in the same way that the idea that health could give life value would be wrong. Or rather, it is wrong unless we understand it to be a kind of tautology, like the one that is involved in the thought that you prefer to survive only if your health is sufficiently good. Just as I think we necessarily value health because we have a physical life, so I think we necessarily value cultural values because it is our nature, as human, to have a cultural life. It is not as if cultural values were something out there that human life (luckily) puts us in the way of, and that then make human life valuable. Nor does Raz think so; in a way that is what creates the problem. Two of Raz's professed theses—that there is no point to values without valuers, and that there is no point to being valuers without value—seem to leave his theory chasing its own tail. We could not coherently care about life only because it provides us with an opportunity to realize cultural values, any more than we could coherently care about survival only because it provides us with an opportunity to be healthy. We have to care about health because we have a physical life. And we have to care about culture because the specific form of human life, of *our* life, is cultural. Here I get some help from Kant.

Kant argues that the fundamental characteristic of humanity is the power to set our own ends. In an essay called 'Conjectures on the Beginnings of Human History'[17] he makes it clear that he does not just mean that reason, in the guise of morality, gives a thumbs up or a thumbs down to the ends proposed by sensibility. Rather, reason, working through a power Kant calls 'comparison', actually proposes new kinds of ends. I have argued, and think it is Kant's view, that self-consciousness is the source of reason. Once you can reflect on the fact that you are inclined to do something, you can ask yourself whether to do what you are inclined to do or not, and then you need a reason. Self-consciousness, and the question it brings with it, creates a problem. Reasons, and ultimately values, are the solution. But this same self-consciousness also creates an opportunity. Kant charmingly makes the point through the story of the Garden of Eden, which he turns into a story about the origin of reason. Human beings instinctively eat certain kinds of fruit—make it pears—but we were not instinctively drawn to those fateful apples. Rather, Eve noticed that the apples were *like* the fruit she instinctively ate, and perhaps also that some creatures who did eat the apples were *like* her. Reflecting on these comparisons, Eve had the first new idea in history: 'You know those apples,' she says to herself, 'I could eat one of those.' Kant says, when this happened, man 'discovered in himself an ability to choose his own way of life without being tied to any single one like the other animals'.[18]

In other words, when we became free and rational, we also became cultural. We can, and necessarily do, devise different ways of life, and

---

[17] In *Kants gesammelte Shriften*, the standard Prussian Academy edition of Kant's works (Berlin), vol. viii. In English translation by H. B. Nisbet in *Kant: Political Writings*, 2nd edn., ed. Hans Reiss (Cambridge: Cambridge University Press, 1991), 221–34.

[18] *Kants gesammelte Shriften*, viii. 112; *Kant: Political Writings*, 224.

choose among them. Notice there are two aspects to culture so understood. First, we devise different ways of carrying out the activities we share with the other animals—eating, finding mates, raising families, and so on. All animals perform those activities, but the other animals perform them in biologically determined ways; while we generate a whole range of different possible ways, which characterize different cultures. Second, we develop totally new kinds of activities, activities in which the other animals do not engage at all—the activities associated with the fine arts, scholarship, science, religion, and generally Raz's 'socially dependent values'. The need for reasons and values arises from the problem posed by self-consciousness, and culture arises from its solution. Cultural life just is the human form of life.

So I do not think it is quite right to suggest that socially dependent values give value to life. I think that it is right instead to say this: given that human beings must lead a cultural life, we must care about the excellences of a cultural life, in much the same way that, given that we must lead a physical life, we must care about health, the excellence of a physical life. I do not mean for that 'must' to convey the idea that cultural values are not sources of joy. I mean instead to be proposing an explanation why these values are, for us, *necessarily* sources of joy, just as physical excellences are. But cultural values do not give value to life, as if from outside. They are simply the excellences of human life itself.

It is possible that I have misunderstood Raz here, and am therefore being unfair. I am taking Raz to be making the same point when he says that the point of being a valuer is realized only when one is exposed to values and when he says that values give life meaning. If so there is another problem here, resting in the fact that the first formulation refers to both good and bad values and the second mainly to good ones. That is, on one way of understanding the idea that the point of being a valuer is realized in valuing, good and bad values are equally involved. It is a shame to be human and fail to love beautiful things, but it is also a shame to be human and fail to be offended by ugliness and vulgarity, or say to hate injustice. A life lived without friendship is hardly recognizably human; but so is a life lived without outrage, contempt, resentment, and grief. One's capacity for valuing is equally expressed and realized in responding to the good, the bad, and the deprivation of the good. But it seems that a human life could not be graced by disdain for the ugly in the way perhaps it can by a love of the beautiful.

To be clear, Raz is not guilty of holding that socially dependent values give value to valuers, or people, in this sense: he does not think that you have to realize cultural values in your life in order to be worthy of moral respect and consideration. He only wants to claim that you need values to realize the *point* of being a valuer. One might say in the same spirit that you need healthy physical activity to realize the point of having a physical life, and that seems right. But Raz does not seem to notice the importance of the resulting asymmetry. I will have to ask my reader to hang on tight here, for the Nietzschean language is about to get completely out of hand. The asymmetry is that valuers are valuable whether or not their point is realized, while values are valuable only if their point is realized. When I say that Raz does not see the importance of that, I mean that Raz seems to think that this issue about the moral value of valuers is just a separate point, orthogonal to his view. But it is not; there is a reason for it. The value of values comes from valuers, and not the reverse, and that fact—that we are the source of value—is also what makes us worthy of moral consideration. Humanity, not the standards implicit in social practices, is the ultimate source of value.[19]

---

[19] Despite the way it sounds, I do not mean to deny that the other animals are sources of value, although I think that their status as such depends on us—we must see them as sources of value. For a discussion of these matters, see Korsgaard, *The Sources of Normativity* (Cambridge: Cambridge University Press, 1996), lecture 4, sects. 4.3.6–4.3.10.

The Conditions of Value

ROBERT PIPPIN

Raz defends the social dependence of values and value pluralism. His main claim is that he has done so without falling into an obvious danger—a relativism about value. His first argument consists in narrowing the scope of the social dependence claim (it will apply only to 'intrinsic', 'cultural' values and not to what he calls 'enabling' values, like freedom, or to most moral values), and by limiting the claim itself to an 'existence' claim (thus denying that the dependence thesis can show that a value's status as a value depends on it being valued at some time by some group). His second argument concedes a certain kind of incommensurability among values, but only a sort linked to our finitude and so not a sort that would have it that there are equally good reasons for valuing some sort of state or object as there are for valuing something like its opposite. With this in place, Raz can show how disagreement about value can often be best understood as interpretative, rather than principled, and so that sustainers of different values can 'both be right', de-fanging, as it were, the anxieties that can arise from ethical disagreement.

This approach eliminates by stipulation quite a lot of controversy, and narrows by stipulation the relevant controversies remaining. I want to suggest why those eliminations and narrowings are problematic and that what we are left with remains ambiguous.

SOCIAL DEPENDENCE

One can be a value relativist for all sorts of reasons. Some philosophers worry about normative language and its ontological commitments, and, because of some theory about language and such commitments, feel compelled to opt for a strong kind of anti-realism in ethics. They fear weird properties or superfluous entities. According to this view, to act well, or rightly, is merely to satisfy the criteria held at a time by some social group, criteria sustained by practices of rewards and punishments, praise and blame. Others are motivated by a sceptical view. They have no direct quarrel with many of the assumptions that Raz has defended elsewhere—that free or intentional action is action based on reasons, and that these reasons are necessarily linked to some notion of the human good or at least specific good-making characteristics of action or ends. But these relativists think that is all just an immensely frustrating counterfactual, only what a non-relativist position would look like. They think that the power of reason to adjudicate differing value claims or establish any such value claim runs out far short of success

Finally, in historical terms, views like value relativism are understood to be due to the work of the likes of Herder originally, and then Nietzsche and Max Weber. Travelling in this company brings us closer to the relativist Professor Raz is addressing, the 'social relativist' about values. Relativists in this group are greatly impressed by the results of modern historiography, social psychology, and cultural anthropology, and by the great flood of information over the last few hundred years about the ways in which peoples in various, differing circumstances observe fundamentally different normative constraints. Diversity and plurality of values alone are not of course on their own reasons to be sceptical about norms, but any reflective person faced with such evidence might well begin to doubt the claims to binding authority with which the values of her own supposedly advanced tribe are asserted.

I do not consider myself a social relativist about values, but I think I know where such a relativist would begin to fidget uncomfortably in listening to Raz's first lecture. Raz wants to defend a thesis freely conceding a premise dear to a relativist's heart—the social dependence of values—but to claim that such a concession does not relativize the validity of those ('intrinsic', 'cultural') values that depend for their existence on a society's 'sustaining practices'. On the face of it, this is quite reasonable and a general, valuable aspect of much of Raz's double-edged work on the limitations of reason and the contingency of value, on the one hand, but for objectivity and against relativism and reductionism, on the other.[1] It *is* extremely unlikely that the idea that gender equality in work roles is of great value somehow just reflected the rational structure of things, and was waiting to be discovered until the last half of the twentieth century; that we simply had incorrect moral views and came to have correct ones. (It was very likely 'waiting', if we can continue that metaphor, for the sorts of complex social structures that could sustain such an aspiration. The same with gay marriage, transnational claims of human rights, or the values of operas, novels, and the like. Indeed, it seems hard to take seriously any philosophical account of such a value that assumes it could always be deduced by pure practical reason alone, or that ignores the value's obvious historicity. On the other hand, such a claim does not seem equivalent to claims about fashion or taste, as if such values belong with rap music, tattooed bodies, and stiletto heels.)

As with so much in philosophy, it all depends according to Raz on what one means by 'sustaining practices' and what one means by 'depends'. I think that there are three different questions to raise about Raz's position, however briefly: (1) just how do values depend on social practices, (2) what, according to Raz, does the answer to (1) establish about values and their validity, and (3), most importantly, has the relativist misunderstood this relation (between (2) and

---

[1] Compare, for example, his argument in chapter 6 of *Engaging Reason* that the necessity of using 'parochial concepts', concepts that cannot be shared or understood across communities or time, does not of itself undermine the possibility of objectivity. We may be picking out various aspects of reality, even if those aspects would not be of much interest in, or play much of a role in, another community (*Engaging Reason* (Oxford: Oxford University Press, 2000), 139).

(1)) , or *is* the relativist mistake essentially or at least typically to draw the wrong conclusions from the social dependence thesis?

(1) The key move is an argument for a more careful classification of the social dependence thesis. It is true, Raz admits, that 'values depend on valuers', that something cannot be a value unless it is or has been valued, that values do not 'exist' unless they are sustained by actual social practices (or have been), and so forth.[2] But these claims about the social dependence of values concern the question of the existence of values. It is a 'metaphysical thesis' ('if you like') about the unique kinds of things values are. They are the kinds of things that must be sustained by a practice in order to be.[3] Further, given the way that Raz understands values (that they are constituted by standards for their success), this claim also means that what counts as the 'excellence' or best realization of such a value also depends on the rules of some social practice. None of this, though, concerns the actual value-making characteristics of the value, or touches the question whether those who are sustaining them and pursuing this excellence ought to be doing so. (For example, what it is for a society to value, aesthetically, small feet is unintelligible apart from the foot-binding practices that constitute the value, and the

[2] As these phrases indicate, Raz's position involves a double qualification on the social dependence thesis. Only the 'existence' of values (not their value status itself) depends on changeable, contingent social practices. (I note that this stipulation alone severely restricts the range of historical interlocutors in philosophy to whom Raz's case might apply.) This might suggest, though, that, when the social practices cease, the values would not 'exist' any longer either. But Raz denies this, and claims that the existence of values depends on social, sustaining practices having at least for a time sustained such a value.

[3] I am not sure how limited or full on a 'metaphysical thesis' Raz intends this to be, since later in the lecture he seems to shift from existence claims (and their conditions) to claims about the 'pointlessness' of talk about values with no social practices to sustain them. A value can thus in some sense exist as an 'unfulfilled' value, thus belying the claim that actual or past social practices are conditions for existence *tout court*, but this is not a telling point for Raz, since arguments about such abstract possibilities are said to be 'pointless'.

standards of success built into such practices. The value came into existence with the practice. And all this is true, even though we can go on and argue that the practice and perhaps the value itself are morally repugnant.[4])

Such social conditions are then 'necessary conditions' for the existence of values, not sufficient conditions.[5] It is also the case that people hold these beliefs for various reasons, and these reasons can be assessed in what Raz believes are the unproblematic, 'ordinary' ways in which such practical reasons are assessed. So at most the dependence thesis will establish a certain anti-utopian limitation on what it is useful to argue about. Values do depend on social conditions for their possible existence, and so we should not waste our time arguing about the worth of institutions that could not be sustained. But when we are arguing about those that could, we will be arguing not about those conditions, but about the merits of the value claims, and this in the usual way.

Parenthetically, we might raise the question of how politically and socially conservative Raz's position might be. (I mean 'conservative' in the sense identified with Burke, Tocqueville, Oakeshott, and so forth.) This question arises because, even though Raz's 'separation thesis'—distinguishing between explanation of the existence of value and evaluation—would allow 'for radical criticism of social practices',[6] that criticism would appear bounded in a way by the results of the social dependence thesis, and bounded in a way that suggests that the separation of social explanations of value, from first-person evaluation itself, is already breaking down. There *are*

---

[4] Cf. the very clear summary of the position, 'Mixing Values', chapter 8 of *Engaging Reason*, 188.

[5] I note that we also need from Raz a clearer picture of what counts as a sustaining 'social practice'. If two people form a (small) cult and begin to treat all animals as of exactly the same moral status as persons, is that all we need to say to justify the claim that the 'necessary condition' for such a value thereby 'coming into existence' has been satisfied? If only one person proclaims and begins to live out the value, does that change anything?

[6] 'The Value of Practice', chapter 9 of *Engaging Reason*, 211.

apparently normatively relevant consequences to be drawn from the social dependence thesis: there are some values about which it is 'pointless' to argue; proposing new values without due attention to context and realizability can lead to 'fanaticism'; and the social dependence thesis 'points to caution in understanding the contribution of such revolutionary innovations' (p. 58).[7] (Indeed, in *The Morality of Freedom*, Raz goes so far as to say about the ideal of autonomy that 'its suitability for our conditions and the deep roots it has by now acquired in our culture *contribute to a powerful case for this ideal*' (emphasis added).[8] *This* kind of 'case' for the ideal again seems to draw together the two elements in 'accounting for value' that Raz appears to be trying to hold apart.)

Now the fact that such caution and demand for sensitivity to context were often invoked as arguments against civil-rights legislation or integration does not of itself establish anything. But we should note that 'social dependence' and derivative claims about 'pointlessness' are close to familiar, cautionary invocations of 'tradition', and so we should also note that fear of fanaticism can have this other side, potentially a hedging, socially regressive timidity. Or at least Raz's formulations make it sound like normatively relevant conclusions are being drawn. Perhaps in this context his own separation thesis should be more strictly observed.[9]

And obviously our relativist will already be objecting here, since, as noted before, she will see no good reason to treat our criteria for assessing an evaluative claim about values in any special or non-socially dependent way. These criteria about what sort of values we should have, and how to go about settling disputes about them, are or

---

[7] Cf. 'The Value of Practice', 210: 'The social basis of value drops out of sight when justification is concerned and plays no role in it at all.'

[8] *The Morality of Freedom* (Oxford: Oxford University Press, 1986), 370. See also p. 394, where autonomy is called a 'fact of life' in our society, and where this fact is appealed to to defend a claim that 'we' cannot therefore prosper at all without autonomy and its conditions.

[9] For more on the issue, see his remarks in 'The Value of Practice', 208–9.

presuppose values too, and much of the hubbub in the last hundred years (from Nietzsche and Weber to Foucault) has been primarily about *them*, about the relativity of what makes a claim about value a 'good' or justifiable instance of such a type and about the self-satisfaction and contingency of institutional claims to embody rational, progressive values. Raz wants to deny this extension of the dependency thesis, to limit the scope of the dependency thesis to 'cultural' values of great importance in a life having a substantive value, and also to exempt from any dependence or relativism claim what he calls 'enabling conditions' for the pursuit of *any* value, 'conditions' such as freedom and much of morality.

Raz of course admits that, were there a society in which it was impossible or extremely difficult for there to be practices that could sustain very many or any individual cultural values, then a value clearly a general condition, an enabling value, for any pursuit of something meaningful, like freedom, although in general exempt from the social dependence thesis, would not be of much value, and so is indirectly subject to the social dependence thesis. Even the moral duty to respect others as ends in themselves would not have much of a point if persons could not realistically act as subjects of their own lives, and so even morality is subject indirectly to the social dependence thesis. And there are certainly other reasons for suspecting complications in any exemption of freedom from such a claim about dependence. For one thing, the interpretative question (what *is* freedom?) is quite complicated and obviously historically sensitive.[10] In the nineteenth century alone, at various times, it looked like I could be said to be free if I had set a goal myself on the basis of reasons (freedom as autonomy of a sort); if I had psychologically identified wholeheartedly with the end (freedom as authenticity or non-alienation); if I precisely had not identified with any role, and

---

[10] For more discussion of these alternatives, see the very helpful articles by Raymond Geuss, 'Auffasungen der Freiheit', *Zeitschrift für philosophische Forschung*, 49 (1995), 1–14; and 'Freedom as an Ideal', *The Aristotelian Society*, suppl. vol. 69 (1995), 87–100.

could take on and discard roles the way an actor takes on and discards roles (freedom as irony, as in *Rameau's Nephew* or in Schlegel); if I had the means to achieve some end (freedom as power); if I had experienced no human impediments to my pursuits (freedom as negative liberty); if I had experienced in my striving a development and growth (dynamic self-realization); and if I had experienced the result of my choice as a genuine 'reflection of me' and 'what I really intended' (self-realization in the sense of self-recognition).[11]

(2) So Raz admits something that figures prominently in relativist premises. The idea, say, that the value of a republican state and the standard of excellence for such a state were waiting to be discovered is as implausible as the idea that it is a norm that ought to be adopted everywhere, regardless of whether there are in place the social conditions (like literacy and health) necessary to sustain such a value. This can begin to sound relativistic, but, on Raz's view, beginning to draw such conclusions is the core of the relativist's mistake. If our relativist concludes from the fact that a certain political form can be said to be a value only under certain social conditions, that its *validity as a value* is limited just *to those* living under such social conditions, and especially if she concludes that, because another value, say a fascist state, is sustained by actual social practices involving millions of enthusiastic people, it therefore must *be* a value, at least 'for them', she will have made the relativist mistake noted above. She will have confused necessary conditions of existence with the full conditions of genuine value and so she will have confused necessary with sufficient conditions.

I think that all of this means that Raz wants to admit the possibility of saying 'X *is* a value, but there is no point in discussing it because it could not now be sustained'—as noted, he has a notion

---

[11] This is a somewhat different strategy, as far as I understand it, than that pursued in 'The Amoralist', chapter 12 of *Engaging Reason*, where the attempt is to show that the pursuit of the sorts of non-moral ends that would give a human life meaning would not be intelligible unless the 'moralist's principle' were accepted. The example of friendship and personhood is a particularly clear and convincing one (pp. 384 ff.).

of 'unfulfilled' value—and not be limited to: 'such a putative value simply does *not exist* absent such conditions.' But I am unsure of how to understand the relation between his social dependency claim as a condition of an 'existence' claim, and as a 'condition of "having a point" ' claim.[12]

(3) *Is* this a typical (or perhaps the typical) relativist mistake or confusion? One reaction is obvious. Our relativist will simply claim a stand-off on the most important issues. It does not follow, she would argue, that the failure of the social dependence thesis to warrant a relativist conclusion all by itself establishes anything about the autonomy or non-relativity of value claims. The question simply remains open. I have already mentioned that many relativists and sceptics are more worried about that additional 'sufficient' condition that for Raz would help establish that a putative value really is a value, what he at one point invokes confidently as a 'full recourse to the whole of one's conceptual armoury, information, and powers of argumentation in reaching conclusions as to which practices sustain goods and which sustain evil, or worthless things, which are, perhaps, taken to be good by a population' (p. 25).

But, as noted before, surely what motivates the relativist in modernity is a deep suspicion of precisely this 'armoury'. (For many, and not just relativists, the bullets are blank, the powder wet, the barrels cracked in that old armoury.) Some failure in, or rather some failure of confidence in, the power of reason and argument to determine the worth of possible ways of life or self-fulfilment are what instigate the search for the kinds of social conditions that might help explain these otherwise mysterious and quite varied commitments. Social dependence, in other words, plays a role in the relativist account, but in no significant case does it play the whole or even major role.

A typical example is Freud's *Future of an Illusion*, where the search for a non-evaluative account (in his case psychological and

---

[12] On the possibility of saying that some possible realization of a value 'would have been good' had there been social conditions to sustain it, see 'Mixing Values', 190.

not social) of why this and not that belief is said to be reasonable begins only after it is established that it is very unlikely that people could be said to believe in religious values as a result of reasoning or 'the powers of argumentation'. Indeed, looked at this way, Raz's thesis seems much too sweeping. Surely there are some value claims for which a reductive explanation (one that attends to what people believe are values, but does not look any longer for evaluative justifications) is appropriate. Freud on religion may be a tendentious extreme, but, at some point in investigating a community's attitudes towards, say, polygamy, we will turn (I should think pretty quickly) to explanations couched in non-evaluative terms.[13]

It is true, in other words, that the fact that a value depends for its existence on a sustaining practice does not of itself show that that value's value depends on people thinking it has value. As Raz points out here and elsewhere (not to mention Socrates in the *Euthyphro*), people do not value something *because* they have taken it to have value; it must be the other way around. But that alone does not establish anything like the autonomy of value criteria. All we need to concede in order to defend our non-evaluative account is that the social factors that contribute to, determine the course of, a person's evaluations, are not available to the individual, and do not and cannot function in the reason and argument given for that value.[14] Someone who claims a right to own and transfer vast amounts of property and who appeals to his 'natural right' to do so obviously takes himself to be invoking a reason, not reporting what his community will accept as a permissive reason. But if we think that the odds are great that 'being convinced by the cogency of natural right reasoning' is very unlikely to have motivated our subject's property theory, and especially if we think, for philosophical reasons, that it

---

[13] Cf. Bernard Williams, 'Nietzsche's Minimalist Moral Psychology', in Richard Schacht (ed.), *Nietzsche, Genealogy, Philosophy* (Berkeley and Los Angeles: The University of California Press, 1994), 237–50.

[14] For a fuller account of Raz's reasoning here, see the essay 'Agency, Reason, and the Good', chapter 2 of *Engaging Reason*, and his remarks in 'The Amoralist', pp. 387 ff.

could not, we will not then take the claim at face value. Or when Raz complains that non-evaluative accounts can never capture the 'nuances' of various values and disvalues, cannot make sense of the identity of what falls under evaluative concepts, we should recall that, for the overwhelming majority of people on the planet, their values and disvalues are linked inextricably to religion, and are in fact religious values and disvalues. At some point, continuing to account for their values in their own terms of assessment might begin to look pointless if we believed that there are no such religious values or religious justifications.

Put one final way: it is true that an obsessional neurotic, when asked why he washes his hands every half hour, will not report that that is what obsessional neurotics do. He will say his hands are dirty, and he values cleanliness. And again, at some point, investigating what reasons he has for the pursuit of this ideal will come to look beside the point, and we will begin looking elsewhere, at either what he unconsciously values or what compels him to act this way. (Raz admits that 'we often have knowledge the grounds for which we cannot articulate, or even knowledge the grounds for which cannot be exhaustively articulated',[15] but that just pushes the question back to distinguishing *knowledge* that is like this, from *knowledge claims* that are only apparently knowledge claims, but that, because unsupported, are 'ideological', to invoke a confusing if useful word.)

If this is possible in principle, then Raz's general claim of a category mistake is wrong, and we are just arguing about when and why we would turn to an explanation focused on dietary practices, social evolution, childhood trauma, preservation of privilege, and so on, and not about whether we could.

A final remark on this issue. Raz is convinced that considerations like those just offered would ultimately lead into a position that is self-refuting because, in order to be a 'position' at all, it has to assert

---

[15] 'Mixing Values', 184. For more on the 'automatic' character of rational 'functioning', see 'Explaining Normativity', chapter 4 of *Engaging Reason*, 39–40.

or assume some value that it cannot with any consistency. And he charges that it will render our first-person point of view as evaluators unintelligible. From that point of view *we* must decide what is valuable and act accordingly, and there is no reason to think that what our society has come to regard as valuable, especially if it has come to do so for non-evaluative reasons, will be of any help within such a point of view.

The self-refutation point is a long and complicated one. But, the latter point, that we have not yet understood how to take up fully, as agents, the 'sideways-on' view of ourselves as sentient animals greatly subject to the effects of a long childhood of socialization in a particular culture, seems to me only to establish *that*, that we do not yet know how to do it. Said another way, the fact that, from the agent as opposed to the spectator point of view, we need to treat evaluative terms as autonomous might say as much if not more about the limits of our imagination as about what is the case.

VALUE PLURALISM

Raz has argued that value pluralism need not mean that antinomial value conflicts can be resolved only by either denying that one or the other value claim is valid (and so denying there is genuine value pluralism), or relativizing the value claim to particular groups or times. Values have abstract or generic as well as specific and individual manifestations. Some concrete values are values because they are instantiations of abstract values; some are distinct values because of 'the special mix of values' they are. In all cases though our evaluations are *genre based*, and this is the key point in avoiding the sort of antinomy that might naturally lead to relativism. We can identify the relevant kind or kinds to which the object or activity belongs, and then compare it with the standard of excellence inherent in such a genre. Pointing out this role of genres and the mix of genres in evaluation is important, because it reveals the crucial role of interpretation in our evaluations, and attention to interpretation can help us understand that deep unresolveable disagreement does not (at least not necessarily) challenge the possible objectivity of value. Given the relative looseness of interpretative possibilities, both parties to the disagreement can even be said to be 'right', without fear of contradiction.

On the face of it this seems quite plausible. It is the kind of 'apples and oranges' response to disagreement that we are all familiar with, as when we try to get people to stop arguing on the assumption that one is right and the other wrong. 'You can both be right,' we say, 'if you realize that you are arguing about apples and your partner is arguing about oranges,' if you understand yourselves to be defending good instances of different, even if conflicting kinds.

Moreover, in other contexts, we often get into these sorts of arguments because a value concept can be vague, with 'no common understanding of its application in some cases', where the sustaining practice and its rules 'underdetermines' the application issue (and so where there is sometimes simply no 'right answer' about interpretations). We can thus share a number of views about values and disagree about how elements relate, about degrees of relative importance, and so on. According to Raz, such disagreements even reveal the extent of the *agreement* necessary for them to get off the ground. Given the looseness of fit between 'concepts and the values which depend on them and their sustaining practices', it is entirely plausible that two divergent value claims can both be said to conform to the general norm, and so rightly claim that the norm means both *this*, and, on the other hand, *that*, in this circumstance. It *is* impossible to tell if a 'duck/rabbit' looks more like a duck or more like a rabbit, even though such disagreement is bounded by substantive agreement (it does not look at all like a chicken).

So the spirit in both lectures is a kind of Pascalean wisdom, as in Pascal's famous remark, 'we know too much to be sceptics, but too little to be dogmatists'. And it would be hard to disagree with that overall spirit. I want to execute my responsibilities as a commentator by raising several questions about this project, which I will simply list *seriatim*.

First, a general point. Value pluralists, according to Raz, 'reject the hubris of the moderns who believe that our ways are superior to those of all other human civilizations' (p. 43). The irony here is that, while of course value pluralism *is* in some sense 'our way'—as a value, it is a distinct product of the liberal, democratic, Western, humanistic tradition—and foreign to many others, we most certainly *do* believe it is superior to jingoistic nationalism, the ways of the Taliban, the attacks by Chinese authorities on Falun Gong, and so forth.[16]

Certainly Raz believes it is superior, so I am a little puzzled by this formulation. As is well known, Raz has defended a perfectionist account of the human good, which he identifies as autonomy, one's ability to set one's own ends and chart the course of one's own life, free from coercion and subjection to the will of others, in a context where a plurality of morally acceptable ends and options is available, and he invokes this substantive value as an objective criterion in ranking societies and regimes as superior and inferior. In the last chapter of *The Morality of Freedom*, when Raz confronts the problem for liberal cultures of whether to tolerate illiberal social, religious, or ethnic groups in their midst, he does not hesitate to claim that such illiberal societies are 'inferior' to liberal ones, and to claim that 'the perfectionist principles espoused in this book suggest that people are justified in taking action to assimilate the minority group, at the cost of letting its culture die or at least be considerably changed by absorption'.[17] Raz admits that this is not easy to do, but

---

[16] I should stress that I am *not* claiming that any 'value pluralist' will encounter this problem. It is not at all the converse of the old charge of self-refutation brought against relativism. Value pluralists need not be, and usually are not, relativists. Moreover, it is even less true of the value pluralists whom Raz has selected out to discuss, because they are pretty tame pluralists, arguing for the incommensurability of value only because of finitude (we cannot realize all value, realizing some will damage the chances for others, etc.) and not because of some radical incommensurability in value itself. All I mean to call attention to here is the oddness of Raz's own formulation about 'superiority', given his overall position.

[17] *The Morality of Freedom*, 424.

the principle is clear enough: no value pluralism with respect to the value of pluralism. This is clearer in his book because such a value is connected more clearly with the requirements of autonomy, but in this context, when we are confronted with the apparent advantage of the social relativist in de-legitimating the evils we have become quite rightly sensitive to, colonialism and cultural imperialism, there are very serious limits, given Raz's position, on the extent to which he can invoke the value of *pluralism* to similar results. Most of his arguments against such imperialism would only be largely 'viability' and prudential considerations.

Of course Raz has made it clear that he wants to say that nothing about it '*being* our way' is ever offered now as a *reason* to others or to ourselves in support of any claim about the value of pluralism or about pluralism's being 'superior'. It may have come into existence and been sustained in a distinct tradition, but its claim can now be assessed and evaluated independently of that context. If we ought to respect fundamental differences on value, we ought to because there is no rational justification for interference and suppression, and because of some direct positive claim about the value of diversity, all defended by reason's 'armoury', and those considerations (at least ideally) are the ones that now determine for us (or for anyone) the legitimacy of any value claim about tolerance and pluralism.

But this response rests on Raz's attempt to separate out explanations of the necessary conditions of a value's existence (the social practices that sustain it) from the question of its value status, and to qualify disagreement by contextual and hermeneutic considerations essential to a value's status, while again distinguishing the strictly normative question. (And therewith again he argues that such disagreements need not cast doubt on reason's role in making a case for or against values. Lots of ethical disagreement, he is saying, is an 'apples and oranges' or 'duck/rabbit' sort of disagreement.) I doubt that we can separate these issues so cleanly and have already noted such suspicions above.

Second, *how* important is the interpretative issue in evaluative thinking and disagreement? There is no doubt that sometimes that can amount to the entire issue. (A lapidary example from the rock star Keith Richards at a press conference after yet another arrest on drug charges: 'Now let's get this straight. I don't have a drug problem. I have a police problem.' I think we would agree that, in this case, both sides are right by their own interpretative lights.) But the 'apples and oranges' (both-can-be-right) and the 'duck/rabbit' (there-is-no-simply-right-answer) ameliorations only go so far; and really, in the important cases, not very far. Both defenders and opponents of affirmative action may be responding to a general underdetermination in the way our social practices sustain the value of, guide interpretations of, rights protection, or fair social entitlement, a value they both agree on. But the fact that they agree on the absolute value of rights protection is largely irrelevant when compared with the depth of their disagreement, and the unavoidability of some decision. Our suspicion that reason is incapable of ever resolving the dispute in favour of one side or the other (that the matter is therefore essentially a political contestation, a struggle for power) remains a genuine anxiety. In such cases, when we seem unable to see how a value can be sustained by appeal to reasons when challenged, we are then tempted to be suspicious that reasons (in the standard philosophical sense) could have had anything to do with the value's status and sustenance, also tend to be suspicious of the relevance of the idealized and highly complicated philosophical arguments that might ensue, and so tend to slide into some sort of relativism or scepticism. Raz of course insists in his own way on the 'contingency' of value and the underdetermination of reason. But he means by this the contingent existence of value, that there is no way to predict or manipulate the social practices necessary to sustain some value, and no way to know clearly what the application of some value will mean in some contingent circumstance. But these last two considerations suggest a more radical contingency about what counts as an acceptable justification of a value. The offering, accepting, rejecting, or qualifying of practical reasons is also a social practice, and so subject in some ways to the contingency of social practices. (I should say that, in other articles, like 'Explaining Normativity', Raz makes his own case for the claim that 'reasoning principles are social principles' and so 'evolve' 'in the ways in which social practices generally evolve'.[18] This is another example of a case where the two elements in accounting for value that he wants, as he said, to separate very clearly come together again, *malgré lui*.)

This raises a third problem about the general meaning or import of ethical disagreement. One thing ethical disagreement can show is just what Raz claims: that social practices can underdetermine the interpretations necessary for the application of values and this alone might justify widespread tolerance and commitment to value pluralism. But it could also be a distinct sort of evidence that our deepest ethical practices are not in order, and it could be a kind of evidence quite different from a philosophical assessment, as that is usually understood. That is, such a disorder, manifested in our conflicting practices and interpretative confusions, would seem in some sense to count against the value itself, its status as a value, and not just count as evidence that the application conditions need to be rethought in a new or complicated context. This would be the same sort of consideration evident when someone wants to insist on what is sometimes called 'internalism' in ethical claims. Values function as reasons for action, and so 'people' (now considered as social groups) must be able to act on such reasons, acknowledgement of the values must be able to form part of an explanation of actions within a society as well as for an individual. When this possibility fails, we can either say: that would still be quite valuable, but it has now become irrelevant or

[18] See 'Explaining Normativity', 51. Raz admits in this article that specific systems and norms of good reasoning are 'historical products' and can be criticized and reformed in the light of their imperfections and limitations. But he rejects (rightly I think) the possibility of a wholesale sceptical attack on formal principles and ideals of rationality. See also his 'Notes on Value and Objectivity', chapter 6 of *Engaging Reason*.

utopian, or we can say that acting that way is, objectively, no longer valuable or as valuable. And I think the latter is closer to the mark, or at least I would not want Raz's approach to disagreement to rule this possibility out of court. (Perhaps the classic case here are the attacks on Kant by Schiller and Hegel for his alleged 'rigorism' in his account of duty. This is a large issue but I take it as uncontroversial that they were not just raising questions of viability and feasibility. Their charge was that his picture of moral life required an oddly unacceptable, perhaps inhumane, self-alienation.)

Or another classic case: when Creon and Antigone disagree about the burial of Polyneices' body, about human and divine law, they *cannot* in that context agree to disagree. It would be bizarre to hear a third party intervene and make an 'apples and oranges' point, however true it is that they *are* arguing at cross purposes. The painfulness and unresolvability of their disagreement, the fact that, given what each believes, there is no way to take up and attempt to incorporate some aspect of the other view, indicates that there is something wrong with the formulation and social understanding of the value itself, something basically wrong with the roles of the divine and human, private and public boundaries, in Sophoclean ethical life. There is not something wrong or incomplete about the arguments they present in the play. Or, that a life cannot be led according to such a norm is a challenge to its normative status, not just to its realizability. Whatever this normative condition is, it certainly changes. There are breakdowns and failures in ethical life of a sort that reveal the limitations and inconsistencies in a value claim itself, in its claim to be able to serve as a reason for action. These genuinely normative failures or breakdowns are in most cases not due very much to the pressure of internal or external critique, to the quality or lack of quality of arguments in defence of the old ways. (And if this is true, then a case for the positive value of autonomy will have to have some sort of historical as well as philosophical justification.)

Raz has provided something of a response to this suggested direction throughout both lectures, when he claims that 'the practice is not what explains why the standard of excellence is a standard of excellence. That is explained by reference to ordinary evaluative considerations' (p. 53). Several times Raz chides the social relativist for avoiding what appears to be an implication of his position: that if it is our material historical existence that fully accounts for the values we hold, we would end up simply reporting our value dispositions to each other as if reporting a kind of fate; we could not, under such assumptions, *make* value judgements, at least not unless we relied on the 'ordinary evaluative considerations' that a reductionist wants to eliminate.[19]

This is a vast topic. I want to close by briefly expanding a point made earlier. First, one can hold views about the role that actual ethical life plays in the possibility of value without being either a reductionist, or subject to this paradox. One can concede that people act on the basis of, and make judgements on the basis of, *what they take to be* justifying reasons, while also claiming that individuals are not able to achieve any complete transparency about the meaning of those appeals to justifying reasons, their historical locatedness and limitations, their real motivating power, or any full picture of their rational status. There are paradoxes involved in the claims about self-deceit, false consciousness, ideology critique, and so forth that lie before us in this direction, but I see no reason to shut the door on such options before they get going.

Second, worries like the one just expressed about confusing the first-person and third-person or 'sideways on' points of view stem from an understandable worry about the reflective responsibility of individuals for their values. We do not want to treat each other as merely passively shaped by, and in our practical lives merely expressing, the influences of socialization and habituation, communal mores and roles. This would be to fail to accord each other the appropriate respect, dignity, and worth as the kinds of creatures we are. We are entitled to such respect because the lives we lead *are* due

[19] See also 'Mixing Values', 192–3.

to us, are actively *led* by us. Whatever social roles we inhabit or conventions we act out, we have somehow made them our own; they function as norms and ideals for us that we must actively and with some justification to ourselves and others adopt. They are not just regularities and dispositions.

This is all true but it leaves quite open what it means to have made these possibilities 'our own', and what that reflective responsibility amounts to. I have only time here to express a doubt that we will explain that essential capacity very well if we operate with a strict dualism between ongoing and unreflective social practices, on the one hand, and periodic reflective moments, on the other, governed by what Professor Raz has called a 'full recourse to the whole of one's conceptual armoury, information, and powers of argumentation in reaching conclusions as to which practices sustain goods and which sustain evil, or worthless things . . .' (p. 25). Just as Raz has argued that we should give up 'the rigidity of the division of domains of thought into those that are either objective and entirely governed by the true/false dichotomy, and those that are entirely subjective and are mere matters of taste' (p. 56), I would urge that we give up an equally misleading dichotomy between our actual, historical social practices in all their contingency, on the one hand, and a reflective recourse to a conceptual armoury, on the other.

Relativism, History, and the Existence of Values

Bernard Williams

Raz describes the social dependence thesis (SDT) as 'a metaphysical thesis, about a necessary condition for the existence of (some) values' (p. 26). It does not apply directly to all values, but other values have a connection with those to which it does apply. Raz is anxious to distinguish his thesis from relativism, which holds something to the effect (as he puts it) that 'the merit or demerit of actions and other objects of evaluation is relative to the society in which they take place or in which they are judged'. Or: 'evaluative standards . . . are valid only where they are practised'. Or again: 'what is valuable is valuable only in societies that think that it is' (pp. 16, 17, 18). So let me say a word first about relativism.

RELATIVISM

Raz says that a mild form of relativism is expressed by 'when in Rome do as the Romans do'. I must say that this piece of advice has always seemed to me very bad. For one thing, some things done by Romans—perhaps not so much now, but in earlier times—were pretty beastly. Even apart from that, the Romans may not like you doing what they do. Moreover, you may not be very good at it. But the relevant point is something that these comments illustrate, that this maxim is not an expression of relativism at all. It is an absolute principle applying to everyone, telling them how to behave in certain circumstances: either, narrowly taken, when they are in Rome or, more broadly, when they are away from home.

Another thing that is not relativism is the thesis that the expression or application of a given value may be different in different social circumstances. This is simply common sense and known to everyone. To take a particularly obvious example, what counts as showing respect or insulting someone differs from place to place, but that does not mean that the value of respect for others is itself relative.

The mark of relativism, as Raz's other formulations bring out, is that values are thought to apply only to a group that is picked out just by the fact that they believe that those values apply to them. The group is, basically, not given independently of its value system, though in fact the references to 'different societies' in statements of relativism do often suggest that it is independently given, by (to put it briefly) anthropological isolation. We shall have to ask later some questions about what 'applies to' means in such connections, but for now we can take it to mean this: if a person belongs to a group that does not believe in a certain value, it is not appropriate for anyone to comment on, criticize, and so on that person's activities in terms of that value.

The best thing to say about this doctrine is that it is almost entirely useless. In the majority of cases, as I have put it elsewhere,[1] it is either too early or too late for relativism: too early if two groups have never heard of one another, too late if they encounter one another and the question is not about 'us' and 'them', but rather about a new 'we'. The one exception seems to be that of comments about the (remoter) past; and then it is not a question of saying that the past values were necessarily appropriate or admirable in that place—that would be to apply some of one's own moral comments to them—but rather of not having any external moral comment to make. (This is

[1] In 'Ethics', in A. C. Grayling (ed.), *Philosophy: A Guide through the Subject* (Oxford: Oxford University Press, 1995).

what I have called the relativism of distance.[2]) Even there, it does not apply to all values. Moreover, it is at most an option. There is no logical or semantic rule that rules it out that I should condemn the High Middle Ages for not adequately respecting the principles of the First Amendment: it is simply not a very sensible thing to do. I am not sure how far Raz might agree with that: I shall come back to the question of how his thesis bears on it.

VALUES EXISTING

Raz expresses his thesis, and the whole discussion, in terms of the conditions on *values existing* (at certain places, times, and so on). My problem is that I am not sure what this means. It might be said this is ungrateful of me, since Raz, largely through the SDT, has told us what it means. But this would be to miss the point, because the SDT is supposed to give (in part) the conditions of something we already understand: my problem concerns what it is that the SDT is supposed to explain.

Let us start with the special SDT. This says that, for some values, they exist only if there are social practices sustaining them (SSPs). (Raz has made various helpful distinctions about what an SSP has to be, how explicitly it needs to be related to the value, and so on, and I will not discuss those questions.) So in these cases, we have

(1) If a certain value, *V*, exists, then there are appropriate SSPs.

But this itself can be further explained. For at least some cases of values to which the special SDT applies,

(2) If *V* exists, then there are instances of *V*,

---

[2] In *Ethics and the Limits of Philosophy* (Cambridge. Mass.: Harvard University Press, 1985), ch. 9.

where 'instances of V' means items of the appropriate kind that bear or exemplify V. This is the point that Raz makes when he says that there are no good operas unless there are operas. But in such cases

(3) If there are instances of V, there are appropriate SSPs.

(2) and (3) together imply (1), and this is the point that Raz puts by saying that the excellence of operas, law, and so on 'depend[s] on the very same social practices' as the existence of operas, law, and so on (p. 31).

However, the sense of 'V exists', as it occurs in (1) and (2), involves only the *emergence* of values. Raz says that 'once [such values] come into being, they remain in existence even if the sustaining practices die out' (p. 22). In some of the examples that he gives, it might be thought not that every SSP dies out, but only those that sustain the creation of new examples of the value: thus there are no new Greek tragedies, but Greek tragedies are read, performed in translation, and so on. (It is arguable that opera may be moving into that state.) But presumably there could be cases in which there was not even this much, but only a trace waiting to be revived.

This point might be taken to distinguish, in terms of SSPs, between an emergence condition for the existence of a value, and a continuation condition, in the sense of some different state of affairs that has to obtain if we are to say that the value goes on existing. But it is not clear to me that Raz thinks that there is any need for a continuation condition at all. It may be that he thinks that, once such a value has come into existence, it necessarily remains in existence: that is, so to speak, the metaphysical nature of values, and we do not need any extra conditions to make them continue.

This question carries more with it than may appear. For Raz takes this point, or something closely related to it, to be what distinguishes the SDT from relativism. He says: 'there is no suggestion that what is of value is so only in societies where the value is appreciated, nor that rights, duties, or values exist only where recognized. Once a value comes into being, it bears on everything, without restriction.

But its existence has social preconditions' (p. 22). Much turns here on what is meant by saying that it *bears on* everything. It could be taken to imply—as one might put it—that, once a value has come into existence, not only will it go on existing, but *it is as though it had always existed*. To get a hold on this, and how it relates to the SDT, it will help to turn, now, to values that are not subject to the special SDT. Raz mentions four kinds of such value. I shall consider just one, the value of beauty and grandeur in nature.

NATURE

Here we need to go back to the distinctions made earlier about the relations between the existence of values and SSPs. The case of natural beauty is not subject to the special SDT: in terms of the schema that I set out in the last section, (1) is false. (2), however, is true—if the value of natural beauty exists, there are (at some time) instances of it. The reason why (1) is false is that (3) is false: there were instances of natural beauty before anyone recognized their value or engaged in any social practices in relation to it. Now indeed we say that the mountains were beautiful or sublime before there were any SSPs for that value, such as lyrical descriptions, paintings, photos, tourism, and so on. We say this because we do not want to say that the mountains became beautiful in—let us say—the late eighteenth century. This would imply that the mountains changed. So we use such words as 'beautiful' to apply to just the kinds of things existing at that earlier time as we pick out with them now. Call this practice— in loose relation to a term in the philosophy of language—'using the words rigidly'.

We can compare the case of colours. Even if no creatures in the Jurassic had colour vision, we can say that the plants then were green (if they were); we do not want to say that the plants changed when creatures with colour vision evolved, and we might have a problem in explaining that evolution if we did. However, there is a special feature of this case compared with that of natural beauty. In the case of colour, what would be the alternative to using our terms rigidly? We certainly could not say that the plants were black and white, or that they were colourless: but we have to say something in that dimension, and that seems to exhaust the possibilities. But, in the case of the beauty of the mountains, do we have to say anything in that dimension at all?

Raz says that an important merit, indeed a particularly obvious merit, of SDT is that it solves problems of the cognition of value. But does it? Raz wants to say, as most of us say if we say anything of the sort, that the mountains were already beautiful before the recognition of that value. In the language of values 'existing' or not, this must surely imply that the value already existed: there could not have been instances of a value at that time that did not exist at that time (that is to say, we can equally read (2) from right to left). Now what about the people who did not recognize that value? Early hominids may have been too busy on other things to notice the beauty of the mountains, but what about those early eighteenth-century divines, for instance, who felt that they had to excuse God for the hideous irregularity of the mountains? They did not recognize the value. What do we say about them?

What is important is that we should be able to discuss, understand, perhaps explain, a change in taste that occurred (let us say) at the end of the eighteenth century. But the language of the 'existence' of values does not seem to help at all in doing this. It either gives us no more than the fact that we use our terms rigidly, a fact that it is not hard to understand but that does nothing to answer the interesting questions, or it points us, perhaps, in the direction of saying that it was some kind of cognitive failing on the part of these earlier people that they overlooked these values that existed in their time, and, even if we were to end up saying something like that, it surely should not be forced on us right from the beginning as an approach to the interesting questions.

POLITICAL VALUES

There are other values that do not satisfy (1) in the schema, at least straightforwardly, but that fail to do so for a different reason. Here it is not that (3) fails, but (2): or so one will put it if using the language of the existence of values. What I have in mind are cases in which there are no instances of a value because that value remains something like an aspiration. In particular, I have in mind political values. We attach importance to certain liberal values—human equality, human rights, freedom of expression. In some places, to some extent, those values are recognized, which means that there are SSPs that support and give institutional form to them. We can say, crudely, that in those circumstances there are instances of them. In other places, there are not yet (adequate) instances, but in those places or in relation to them there may be other SSPs, such as protest, that express an aspiration to the realization of those values.

Liberal values have a complex history. Let us say, simplifying wildly, that recognition of them and articulated conscious aspirations to them are something else that came about in the eighteenth century. Now I take it, if I understand the SDT, that Raz wants to say that the values came into existence at that point. But what, on his view, does that mean for our evaluations of the world before that time?

We may recall that, in distinguishing his position from relativism, Raz said that once a value comes into being 'it bears on everything'. As I put it earlier, we might express this thought by saying that, even though a certain value comes into existence at a certain time, from that time on it is as though it had always existed. In any case, I take it that Raz means that we can apply the value to states of the world before that value existed. It is of course true that we can say evaluative things about earlier societies, and some of them are more sensible than others: the thought, for instance (which must have occurred to many who saw the movie *Gladiator*), that the Romans were by any standards notably brutal. But the present question is more particular: whether on Raz's view the specific values of liberal democracy apply to or 'bear on' earlier societies, such as those of the Middle Ages or the ancient world. Presumably the questions whether those values already existed, or did not already exist, or it is as if they already existed, have something to do with this.

What are we supposed to say about these people? It can hardly have been a cognitive failure of theirs, not to recognize a value that did not yet exist. Was it a failing of theirs that they had not brought it into existence? Rather—to make the question more precise—was it a failing of theirs *in terms of that very value* not to have brought that value into existence? Was it a failing of theirs at all that their practices did not accord with these values, as it is a failing in some contemporary societies? Was it even a deficiency of their societies, if it was not yet historically possible for a society to embody these values? If it was not a failing or deficiency of any kind, what is it for the values to apply to them?

Someone might prefer to say that, in the case of values such as these, the value did exist at that time, but it was only recognized later. I do not think that Raz wants to say this, since this way of putting it would make the SDT more restricted than he wants it to be. Someone might say that it is an argument for this way of putting it, that those who first spoke in favour of these values called for their *recognition*: if their words implied anything about the existence of these values, they spoke as though they already existed. But, if we take this seriously, the cognitive problem comes back: what was wrong with the pre-modern world, that it did not recognize these values? Why did the existence of these values, which had always been there, only burst on the world in the eighteenth century?

There are real historical questions here, such as that small historical puzzle, where did the modern world come from, and how? There are also real interpretational and ethical questions: how far is it pointful and helpful to discuss earlier states of the world in terms of our more local values? How local are our values? Certainly, as I have said, there is nothing in the nature of the universe or of language to stop one applying one's values in this way. As I have put it in another connection, you can be Kant at the Court of King Arthur if you want to. The question is the extent to which it is reasonable and helpful to do so, or rather gets in the way of understanding; in particular, of understanding how we differ from the past, and hence who we are. I am not convinced that we are helped in thinking about these things, and I suspect we are hindered, by asking questions about the conditions under which various values *exist*. I do not think we would lose anything if we dropped this way of speaking altogether.

VALUE PLURALISM

In these connections, I very much agree with a point that Robert Pippin makes that a historical and an evaluative enquiry into our own values are not entirely separate from one another. In particular, it is precisely a typically modern self-consciousness about the emergence of our own values that has helped to raise doubts whether they are everything that they claim to be. This is particularly so because they have presented themselves as emerging from a particular kind of historical process, one that validates them, and in a sense validates them universally. This is why I have drawn attention, as Christine Korsgaard also does, to the question of what Raz means by saying that, once a value has emerged, 'it bears on everything'. It raises the question, too, of what is involved in value pluralism, and how it is distinct from relativism.

Now I think that there is a clear and consistent position that Raz can take on these issues; if I am not entirely sure whether it is the position he has taken in his lectures, this is because I am not sure what view he takes of Kant at the Court of King Arthur—that is to say, on what he thinks we can helpfully say about pre-liberal societies. For this part of the discussion, I shall not take 'values' in the broadest descriptive sense, to mean anything that any society can intelligibly recognize as values, but rather to mean values that we ourselves can positively acknowledge. As Raz has said, pluralism thinks that there are various values and that they cannot all be consistently realized in one life or one society. One expression of this is that in political decision there are, as Isaiah Berlin used to put it, inevitable value losses. In rather similar terms, we may be able to say about some past society that it was strong on some value that we can acknowledge, but not on others. This is not relativism, since it says something about that society that goes beyond the values of that society; nevertheless, it allows us to recognize that for some values, including some that are particularly dear to us, it was not a *failing* of that society or the people in it that it did not embody or recognize those values, since it was not yet historically possible to do so.

However, someone might agree with all this, and still say that it was in a certain sense a *deficiency* of that society that it did not embody these values. This would mean that, while it was not historically possible for it to embody or express them, and to value all the things we value, the society was in this respect imperfect or incomplete or underrealized. I take it that there have been basically two versions of this view: roughly speaking, Aristotle, and Aristotle plus history, which is (even more roughly speaking) Hegel. But, as it seems to me, it is precisely a central feature of our actual disenchanted condition that we have no reason to believe either of these stories.

Christine Korsgaard seeks to reanimate the Aristotelian view when she talks about excellence within various genres: the excellence of houses, for instance, or of the state, as determined by human nature. She suggests that the Aristotelian aspiration can have a Kantian outcome: that we may be able to understand the emergence of liberal values as the realization of a potentiality implicit in us as valuers. I find this very hard to believe, and this is not just because I am relativistically resistant to 'a bit of modern hubris'. Rather, in so far as we have a grasp on 'human nature'—and I shall not go into the present condition or possible fate of that concept—a notable fact about it is that it underdetermines ways of human living. This is partly for reasons grounded in evolutionary and social theory. The peculiarity of human beings is their capacity and need to live under culture, and I do not see how it could be that this capacity and need, properly understood, will reveal that human beings are really 'meant to' live under one fairly specific form of culture, that of liberal modernity. Underlying this is a more general issue of principle. If there is such a thing as an essential nature of human beings, there is only one way in which it can rule anything out—by making it impossible. If it has failed to rule it out in that way, it cannot try to catch up by sending normative signals. Such an idea would make sense only if there were more teleology in the universe than is represented by evolutionary adaptation, and one thing we know that Aristotle did not know is that there is not.

The historicized version of the teleological story is also one we cannot or should not accept. Here it is important to remember some quite basic facts of the history of ideas, and indeed just of history: that Hegelianism was a form of idealism, which if it is anything is an inherently teleological conception, and that the heroic attempt to tell a similar story without idealism, Marxism, just failed. Without some such story, it is hard to see how the historical account of the emergence of our values is going to validate them.

If we accept the complete failure of any teleological tale, then it was not even a *deficiency* of those earlier societies not to embody some of our most treasured values: and if that is all there is to be said about it, it is hard to say how our values 'bear on everything'. However, perhaps there are bits to be picked out of the ruins of the Hegelian project, which would help us to say a bit more. A concern with this is the reason why I have pressed Raz on the question of what his model gives us to say about the past. It is also why I agree with Robert Pippin in thinking that the historical and the evaluative enterprise should not be too sharply separated.

Before turning to that, however, I should mention a different matter on which I do not agree with Pippin, and do entirely agree with Raz: this is on the question whether value pluralism runs the risk of being inconsistent, because it must esteem pluralistic societies (notably our own) more highly than others. This idea seems to me wrong. Value pluralism is a thesis about values, not itself a political or ethical ideal. What is true is that the modern world is *conscious* of value pluralism. If you add to this consciousness certain other beliefs, about the value of something like individual autonomy, which indeed figure among our values, you will get beliefs in social pluralism, toleration, and so on, and of course Pippin is right in saying that the liberal cannot consistently regard those as being as much up for grabs as anything else; but Raz would also be right to reply that this was not what he was talking about. What Pippin would need in order to produce an unequivocal ranking of societies in these respects would be the belief that more self-conscious societies were higher or in a better position than others. The idea that this belief is simply given is another teleological assumption: indeed, it is a vital part of the Hegelian teleological assumption.

What we can say, I think, is this. The question whether self-conscious and critical societies are a higher expression of human nature (period) may be unintelligible—messages sent to the Aristotelian essence centre are, as always, returned unopened to the sender. But we have such a society, and we have values associated with that, and there is no road back. I do not mean that there could be no historical process that could lead back—that is certainly false. I mean that we could not consistently set out to go back, not only because of the specific values we have in our present condition, but also because forcing people to go back or trying to do so would involve something not involved in merely *being* back: massive coercion, which offends against many other and highly general values.

There is the further and important point that the legitimation stories offered by many past societies to justify their social orders and the associated values depended on what we can see to be myths. Certainly, many legitimation stories that are told about our kind of social order and its values are equally myths, but a real question certainly remains, of how far we might still hope to honour the Enlightenment ideal of finding a stable and decent form of human community that was (to put it moderately) minimally dependent on myths. In so far as that is a question for theory, part of the answer to it must be found by trying to understand our values and how we came by them, in relation to the values of the past. This is in my view one of the most important issues raised by Raz's lectures.

Reply to Commentators

Joseph Raz

More on Explaining Value: Replies and Comparisons

The privilege of having three sets of extensive and hard-hitting comments on one's work is as welcome as it is rare, and especially so on this occasion as the lectures were, for me, but the first (well, not entirely first) stab at a subject I hope to explore at greater length. The reflections that follow will respond to some of the criticisms, but will not be a point-by-point reply. I will use the occasion to clarify some obscurities in the lectures, and to contrast my view with some of my critics' own positions. I will proceed thematically, starting with some observations about method and about ontology, proceeding to explore several questions about the relations between social dependence and relativism, between genre, value, and normativity, and concluding with a few words on pluralism and liberal values.

METHOD AND ONTOLOGY

My aim is explanation, explanation of concepts that are central to our practical thought, to our understanding of ourselves as persons, capable of intentional action—namely, an explanation of the closely related concepts of value, of being a value, and of having value or being of value. In explaining a concept we explain aspects of that of which it is a concept. An explanation of the concept of value is a (partial) explanation of the nature (that is, essential properties) of value. And, as the difference between explaining concepts and explaining the nature of what they are concepts of is immaterial for the current discussion, I will proceed on the assumption that the lectures aimed at this dual task, which is discharged, for the most part, by the same explanations (often suitably modified to apply either to value or to the concept of value).[1] I make no claim that it is impossible to understand the notions of being a person, or of reason or intentional action, without using the concepts I am trying to explain. It is merely that for those who have them they play a central role in understanding intentions, reason, and persons, and that for those who have them possessing other routes to an explanation of intentions and persons involves understanding how those other concepts relate to the value concepts that are the subject of these lectures. For those who have them, the understanding of intentional action, and of being a person, and of much else depends, among other things, on understanding the interrelations between their concepts and value concepts.

Neither my lectures nor the comments on them embarked on an extended discussion of the methodological assumptions behind the enterprise, and it would be inappropriate to do so here, except to the extent that some methodological issues are pertinent to an evaluation of several critical observations made by Korsgaard, Pippin, and Williams. Before I turn to them, two brief and general remarks regarding the nature of the explanatory task as I see it. First, it is a constructive-theoretical task. It aims at explaining central concepts, concepts that can be compared to crucial links at important junctions connecting central features of our thought, and thus contributing importantly to the structure of our thoughts. But the idea of a concept used in philosophical analysis generally, and mine is no exception, while being recognizably related to 'concept' in its ordinary meaning, deviates from it considerably in pursuit of theoretical

---

[1] On this as on many other points in the lectures and the reply I will be relying on arguments I advanced elsewhere, especially in *Engaging Reason* (Oxford: Oxford University Press, 2000). To avoid tedium I will not refer again to that book. But let me mention that the view of concepts presupposed here is delineated with a little more detail in 'Two Views of the Nature of the Theory of Law: A Partial Comparison', *Legal Theory*, 4 (1998), 249–82, repr. in J. Coleman (ed.), *Hart's Postscript* (Oxford: Oxford University Press, 2001).

aims.[2] It is part of the enterprise of explaining the basic features of human thought, an enterprise that gives concepts a central role in articulating those features. So the explanation of concepts is an explanation of human thought as we know it, using the notion of a concept as a tool of analysis.

I do not assume, and indeed do not believe, that there is a fixed budget of philosophical problems the explanation of which is the perennial task of all philosophy. Rather, I assume that there are indefinitely many philosophical puzzles, different ones gaining prominence at different times, different ones being felt as pressing at different times. The task of explanation is never ending. Still, there are some typical philosophical preoccupations and one of them is the desire to explain the possibility of a unified world view—that is, one where our understanding of any domain coheres with our understanding of all other domains. Many recent writings about practical thought aim at presenting a so-called naturalistic view of practical thought, because the writers believe that the only way to reconcile practical thought with our world view is to show how it can be integrated in a naturalistic world view. I am not confident of the cogency of the ideal of 'a naturalistic world view', but the aim of explaining the coherent relations between our practical thought and other domains of thought is one of the background goals of my lectures.

Do my commentators share this understanding of the task? It may appear that they do not, but matters are not altogether clear. Pippin explicitly criticizes my conception of my own endeavours:

Parenthetically, we might raise the question of how politically and socially conservative Raz's position might be. . . . This question arises because, even though Raz's 'separation thesis'—distinguishing between explanation of the existence of value and evaluation—would allow 'for radical criticism of social practices', that criticism would appear bounded in a way by the results of the social dependence thesis, and bounded in a way that suggests

---

[2] The same is true of the concept of 'the nature of . . .' or of 'essence'. They too are philosophical concepts, used as they are for theoretical reasons, and not identical with the concepts expressed by these words in non-philosophical English.

that the separation of social explanations of value, from first-person evaluation itself, is already breaking down. There *are* apparently normatively relevant consequences to be drawn from the social dependence thesis: there are some values about which it is 'pointless' to argue; proposing new values without due attention to context and realizability can lead to 'fanaticism'; and the social dependence thesis 'points to caution in understanding the contribution of such revolutionary innovations'. (pp. 90–1).

'Separation thesis' is Pippin's coinage, presumably referring to two of my claims. First, that the enterprise I am engaged in is one of explanation of aspects of central concepts like that of a value, and not the enterprise of establishing what values there are, or what is of value and what is not. Second, the more substantive claim that, conventional goods apart, the existence (or absence) of a sustaining social practice is not part of the case for establishing that something, say fraternity, is a value, or that something, say chastity, is not. Neither of these claims is challenged by the, to my mind, correct observations Pippin is making in the quotation above (and related ones elsewhere in his comment).

Pippin seems to me right, and I never denied, that an explanation of a concept can have normative, or evaluative,[3] consequences. It is easy to think of propositions that, if true, are part of an account of (the concept of) value and that have normative implications. For example, it is plausible to think that a reasonably comprehensive, correct account of value will entail either that nothing of value can exist, or its negation—that is, that possibly something of value exists. Or that a reasonably comprehensive, correct account of value will entail either that there cannot be any values, or its negation— that is, that there are some values.[4] Needless to say, if a correct

[3] Except where otherwise indicated I use the terms interchangeably.

[4] Regarding both examples it is possible that neither of the theses would be entailed by an account of the nature of value. But given (1) that an account of a concept (or of the nature of that of which it is a concept) is likely to be informative about the possibility of its instantiation, and (2) that such propositions, central to the understanding of the concept, object, or property in question will not lack truth value, it is plausible to make the assumption I make in the text.

account of value entails either of these propositions, then it has normative implications. It follows that it is possible for a correct account of value to have normative implications, and that it is plausible to think that any reasonably comprehensive correct account has such implications. There are many other normative implications that correct accounts of value have, and it is impossible to enumerate or exhaustively describe their general character independently of knowledge of the content of that account.

There are other ways, of course, in which a correct understanding of the nature of value can quite properly affect people's normative views. People's views are often based on or supported by confused notions of the nature of value, whose dissolution will help people to avoid making evaluative mistakes.

Perhaps I should add here that there is another separation thesis that my lectures do not entail, and that I believe to be unfounded. Some people may hold that, while a correct account of the nature of value is likely to have normative implications, its cogency cannot be properly supported by evaluative considerations. A more plausible version of this view distinguishes between normative considerations that apply specifically to theory construction and other normative considerations. It claims that only the first kind of normative considerations bear on the cogency of accounts of value, but not the second kind. I do not believe that this exclusion or separation can be sustained. Our understanding of the nature of value inevitably derives in part from what we take to be obvious or clear cases of values: freedom, beauty, and so on. I do not mean that our view that this or that is a clear case of a value cannot be revised, or that it cannot be revised in the light of an improved understanding of the nature of value. Such revisability is consistent with the fact that part of the case for any account is that this or that is a clear or obvious case of value. Hence evaluative considerations do legitimately count in favour of the account of the nature of value. We are very far from affirming the separation thesis that Pippin rejects.

Pippin points to several considerations that he takes to be inconsistent with the separation thesis. One of them is that there can be successful reductive explanations of value claims: 'Surely [he writes] there are some value claims for which a reductive explanation (one that attends to what people believe are values, but does not look any longer for evaluative justifications) is appropriate' (p. 95). And to be sure there are such cases (though I do not think that the explanations involved are reductive). My claim was that the correctness of 'value claims' can be established only by appeal to other value claims (though one may appeal to the circumstances in which people acquired their evaluative beliefs to establish the probability that they are correct: they may have had reliable teachers, and so on). The same is true of establishing that people's evaluative beliefs are unfounded. That too can be established only by appeal to evaluative considerations (if only because establishing that an evaluative belief is mistaken often amounts to establishing that its negation—also an evaluative belief—is correct). However, here too there is room to appeal to the circumstances in which the belief was acquired or held to explain why a mistaken belief appeared credible. Such explanations of error are particularly pressing when the mistaken belief is widespread and the circumstances in which it is held make it difficult to accept that everyone could have been mistaken. Such doubts may undermine the credibility of (evaluative) arguments to establish that it is mistaken. Explanations of why the error occurred, how the erroneous view could have seemed plausible, and so on are, therefore, valuable in reinforcing the evaluative arguments against the views concerned.

On occasion the circumstances under which a view is held may be such as to undermine the credibility of those who hold it thus. Given those circumstances, we may deny that they are reasonable to hold it, even when we do not know why the view is implausible, or what is wrong with the reasons (if any) that those who hold it think they have for it. In these cases, explanations of why the belief is held do all the work: we may have no other reason to doubt the belief but, knowing that it is held because . . . , we cannot have any faith in it. We realize that we would hold it whether or not it was true, that our belief is not sensitive to its truth; that it is immune to critical-rational control and will not change in response to rational consider-ations only. Therefore that it cannot be trusted.

It is possible that Pippin and I agree or at least that we do not dis-agree, it is possible that he said nothing inconsistent with my view on the relationship between explanation of value and justification. If so, then how 'politically and socially conservative' is my position? When the phrase is used in its main meaning, being conservative is not a matter of rejecting or affirming any value. Rather, it is a matter either of epistemic caution in concluding that one understands the values correctly (that is the context of my observation about fanatic-ism to which Pippin refers) or of minding the possible adverse con-sequences of a single-minded pursuit of some values, of not allowing oneself to be blinded to the relevance of other values. In its second-ary meaning, 'being conservative' means supporting certain sub-stantive evaluative views—that is, those that are at the time of speaking thought of to be such as are predominantly supported by people who are properly or excessively conservative (depending on the speaker's own views on these matters).

Pippin points to various ways in which some of my observations can be used in support of conservative caution. But at no point does he either allege or show that they can *correctly* be used to support wrong views. Perhaps his reticence is just a matter of politeness, but it is important nonetheless. There is nothing in the social depend-ence thesis, or in my arguments for it, that supports the status quo and opposes change, or that supports 'traditional values'—say, traditional ideals of the family—and opposes 'new values'—say, values that sanction non-traditional forms of personal relation-ships. Besides, I am not sure that my position is relevant to the con-cerns he gestures towards. One does not need to accept the social dependence thesis to argue cogently that 'there are some values about which it is "pointless" to argue' or that 'proposing new val-ues without due attention to context and realizability can lead to "fanaticism" '. These are vague, but so far as they go sound points to make, the merit of which is visible to all, whatever their understanding of value.

I will revisit these and related matters when commenting on 'liberal values' and the like. For the time being let me return to the question whether we all share the same understanding of the enterprise we are engaged in. Williams, for example, writes: 'I am not convinced that we are helped in thinking about these things, and I suspect we are hindered, by asking questions about the conditions under which various values *exist*. I do not think we would lose anything if we dropped this way of speaking altogether' (p. 114). When the enterprise is explanatory, one may think, the advice 'let's drop this way of speaking' is out of place. Does that not show that Williams is engaged in a different enterprise? But as usual things are not that simple. Is Williams advocating conceptual reform? This is not clear, but if he is what could be the grounds for such reform? Conceptual reform can be a result of analysis that uncovers incoherence in our concepts (the classical example, however controversial its success, is Russell's revision of the concept of a set to avoid his own set paradox). It could also be a result of analysis that establishes incongruence between the presuppositions underlying the use of some concepts and fundamental aspects of our world view. Williams has argued in other publications that values do not belong to the absolute conception of the world. I joined others in expressing doubts about his views on the subject. These do not matter here. What matters is that I agree that philosophical analysis that points to such incongruities in our basic concepts opens the way to conceptual change. So there is no clear evidence here that my enterprise is any different from Williams's.

Very likely Williams recommends no conceptual revision in the quoted remark. He may simply mean that certain ways of framing the quest for explanation are unhelpful, and may lead the unwary to accept false assumptions about values. If the advice is addressed to the ways we express ourselves in ordinary, or most philosophical discussions of evaluative matters, including arguments about the value of this or that, then I completely agree. We do not often talk in these words about the existence or non-existence of values, nor is this to be regretted. My defence of discussing the dependence of value on practice in terms of existence conditions has to do with another way in which use of the term 'value' in theoretical discussions deviates from its standard English meaning.[5] The reason is that there we are interested in a broad category of evaluative properties, whose explanation has much in common, and there is no common term in English to cover all of them. Values are what those that possess the evaluative properties have in virtue of their possession. Their possession of value is what we are trying to explain, as well as the relation between the general possession of value and the specific nature of the properties that endow their possessors with value—that is, the relation between having value in general and being a value of a specific kind is part of the explanatory task.

Given that it is justified to use, in theoretical enquiries, 'value' in this partly stipulative broad sense, talk of the existence of values is both inevitable, and inevitably odd-sounding on many occasions. It sounds odd, for using a standard philosophical jargon I sometimes talk of the existence of values, and so on, where normally we would talk, and that does not sound odd at all, of the question whether there are values, whether something is a real value (or really a value), and so on. I have no desire to see the use of 'existence of values' locutions spread. Yet they are sometimes helpful in sharpening and in forcing distinctions in answers to the inevitable questions that I discuss. The question of the existence of values arises in ordinary—that is, non-theoretical—discourse, as well as having a systematizing role in theoretical discussions. The concept of value is such that claims such as 'some people believe that piety is an important value, but in fact it is not a value all', 'the belief that values are universal is false. There are no universal values', 'not all reasons derive from values', whether true or false, are meaningful, and import questions that in the standard

---

[5] I remarked on this in the lectures above.

philosophical jargon can be expressed by reference to the existence or otherwise of values.

Some would deny that in explaining claims such as those we need to refer to values. Korsgaard is among them. She believes 'that talk of the existence of values at this level is just misleading shorthand for something else—namely, valuing, which is a thing that we *do*' (p. 68). She is right that often reference to values is best seen as a reference to what people do, or may, value. For example, 'modesty is an old value, whereas independence is a new one', 'Aztec culture was unique in having embraced so many false values', 'middle-class values are very different from working-class values' are best understood to state that people have long valued modesty, whereas only relatively recently did they come to value independence, that the Aztecs valued many things that were of no value at all, and that in general people of the middle class value different things from working-class people. Yet I think that she is wrong in thinking that such paraphrases apply everywhere and enable us to do away with the thought of values. This is so primarily because valuing can be right or wrong and it is right or wrong depending on whether what is valued possesses or fails to possess the value property because of which it is valued, or at any rate some value property in virtue of which its valuation is right, or in the absence of which it is wrong.

Observations such as the preceding one lead many to the view that discourse about values simply refers to evaluative properties—that is, properties possession of which necessarily endows their possessors with some value.[6] Discourse about beauty is about the property of being beautiful, and so on. I think that every value correlates to a specific evaluative property. However, considerations of the temporal dimensions of value advanced in the lectures suggest that values cannot be identified with their corresponding properties, since properties do not have a temporal dimension. In other words, consid-

---

[6] There may be a case for broadening the category of evaluative properties beyond those captured by this characterization. But for present purposes it will do.

eration of the existence of values is required not so much to explain locutions such as 'the value ... exists', but in order to explain the relations between values that govern and partly constitute genres, and the genres that they govern, which beyond doubt have a temporal dimension. This is but one of a range of considerations forcing on us recognition of the temporal dimension, and therefore (in order to make sense of it) recognition of the existence of values. Another consideration will be mentioned below, as it is relevant to the relationship between the social dependence of value advocated here, and social relativism.

ONCE A VALUE COMES INTO BEING, IT BEARS ON EVERYTHING, WITHOUT RESTRICTION

Pippin correctly remarks that: 'Our relativist will simply claim a stand-off on the most important issues. It does not follow, she would argue, that the failure of the social dependence thesis to warrant a relativist conclusion all by itself establishes anything about the autonomy or non-relativity of value claims' (p. 94). It was not my aim to refute any version of evaluative relativism, and I presented no arguments at all against any version of relativism. I contrasted my view with a broad family of relativistic alternatives (never precisely characterized in the lectures) first to help the reader see that my view differs from theirs, and second to show how some of the reasons that prompt people to endorse versions of social relativism can be satisfied in an account that is not relativistic.

There is no simple summary of the way my view is not a relativistic one, if only because there are so many different versions of relativism, and my account diverges in different ways from different versions. Indeed, there is nothing to stop someone from defining a version of relativism of which my account is an instance. After all, I believe that values are—generally speaking, and subject to exceptions and modulations—dependent on social practices. I take that claim to be at the heart of social relativism. Perhaps the crux of the difference between my account and social relativism, in all its varieties, is that, according to the view I explained in the lectures, (1) four important types of value—pure sensual and perceptual pleasure, aesthetic value of natural phenomena, many enabling values, and the value of people and others who are of value in themselves—are at most indirectly dependent on social practices and (2) once a value comes into being, it bears on everything, without restriction.

That last sentence merits further explanation. As Williams points out, I take a sustaining social practice to be 'an emergence condition' for the existence of a value, not 'a continuation condition'. The reasons are many. Here is one, which I regard as particularly forceful.[7] Many values are mixed values: the value of being a good opera consists in the way visuals, music, words, and action, each with its own forms of excellence, combine. As explained in the lectures, we can think of a value as defined by, or constituted by, a standard of excellence of a certain type.[8] Since many values are mixed values, their standards of excellence refer to other values, and their required combination makes the values they define distinctive.[9] They are distinct because whatever possesses this complex mixed value excels in a way other than simply by possessing the component values. The whole is greater than the sum of the parts—that is, the value of the whole is greater than its value measured by the sum of the component good-making properties it possesses. The thought sounds complicated but is elementary: a good film is good in ways other than as a collection of good photos, a collection of funny episodes, and so on. The way they combine determines its value as a film, which is different from its value as a collection of good shots, good jokes, and so on. Hence,

[7] I relied on it for the first time in 1991 in a paper that is now chapter 8 of *Engaging Reason*.

[8] I will discuss Korsgaard's objection to this point below.

[9] To avoid misunderstanding, or the kind of slippage that, according to Korsgaard, I am guilty of in the lectures, let me clarify that mixing values means possessing the respective value properties, and possessing them in the right relationship, as required by the values in question. Where the meaning is clear I spare the reader such complicating clarifications.

being a good film is a distinct good-making property corresponding to the value of films.[10]

The crucial step in the argument is that any combination of values can constitute a distinct value. That is, that there are no combinatorial principles that dictate that only certain ways of combining values can be required by standards of excellence, and other combinations are ruled out: they cannot constitute distinct complex mixed values. If that is accepted, and I will not argue for it here, it follows that there could be as many values as possible combinations of values—that is, an indefinite number. We know, however, that not all those possibilities represent real values, not every possible combination is a distinct value. For example, one can criticize an object, say a film, for having the right components but failing to integrate them well. Sometimes such criticism can be met by pointing out that it mistakes the genre the film belongs to: it would be justified had this been a psychological drama, but it is a romantic comedy, and the elements are well integrated because they are related as they ought to be for a good romantic comedy.

If there were as many distinct values as possible combinations of values, it would never be possible to criticize a film, or anything, for failing to integrate its elements well, for there would always be some other value that it exemplifies to a high degree.[11] But this is nonsense. We cannot refer to any possible way of relating component

[10] Notice that here, as elsewhere in the lectures and in this reply, I use examples loosely. I do not stop to consider whether 'film' designates a kind partly constituted by a distinctive form of excellence, or whether that is true of storytelling films, documentary films, etc., but there is no larger genre 'film' marked by its own distinctive excellence.

[11] I am assuming, of course, that the value applies to the instance in question. Since these values will most likely be kind based, this implies that the instance will be of the relevant kind. This assumption is based on the thought that items can be instances of a number of kinds, and that there could be different kinds, differing only in what constitutes excellence in them, whose condition of membership of the kind is that the item be better if it belongs to that kind than if it belongs to any other. That means simply that it belongs to the kind if it excels by its standard more than by any other standard of excellence.

values as a value, only a subclass of combinations is a value. The social dependence thesis claims that only those that, at some point, were supported by a sustaining social practice are existing values, only they can justify actions, emotions, and so on in the ways that values can. Two factors combine to give sustaining social practices the role of emergence conditions, to borrow Williams's term. First, the crucial assumption I mentioned above was that there are no evaluative considerations that can determine which combinations of values are a distinct value. Social practices meet the bill, for they are concrete facts, rather than evaluative considerations. Second, they make the contours of the value learnable and graspable by people, they concretize a standard of excellence making it available for people to learn and be guided by. Hence, the special social dependence thesis can explain how some possible standards of excellence, some possible combinations of values, are distinct values and others are not. It explains it in a way consistent with our conceptual practices, with the way in which we distinguish legitimate valuations and illegitimate ones.

Once a sustaining social practice comes into being, and the value emerges, there is no reason to think that it will not continue to exist if the practice dies out. It has been concretized through the practice, which can be learnt about and understood even after it no longer exists. Moreover, we do actually refer to such values, whereas we do not refer to pure possibilities as values.[12]

Grant, therefore, that cultural values, for they are the important type of value subject to the special social dependence thesis, depend on social practice for their emergence, but not for their continued existence. In what sense do they, once they exist, bear on everything without restriction, since that is meant to be an important difference between this view of social dependence and the standard social-

---

[12] This point has to be qualified to allow for the deliberate efforts of people to innovate and create new genres with their attendant values. I will not delineate the ways such innovative discourse differs from the invocation of existing old values. The differences should be familiar to the observant reader.

relativistic view? The answer is in what has just been granted. To use Williams's terminology again, sustaining social practices constitute emergence conditions, and not—as they do according to standard social relativism—application or validity conditions.

Social relativism is not to be confused with the claim that cultural values are genre based. Korsgaard asks whether buildings on Mars realize the values of classical architecture. They may possess the component properties that contribute to excellence in the classical style, such as symmetry, serenity, and solidity. There is no problem in asking about any building whether it is serene, symmetrical, or solid. The view that cultural values are broadly genre-dependent claims, however, that to possess the values of classical architecture a building has to belong to the classical style. Membership of a genre, being an instance of the classical genre in this case, is determined in ways that may be (but need not be) independent of how it would excel by the standard of the style were it an instance of it. Only buildings in the classical style can excel in the classical virtues (allowing that buildings of other styles can be marginal cases of two styles, refer to other styles than their own, and so on and so forth).[13]

Korsgaard seems to take this to show that my view is relativistic after all. That conflates genre-based evaluation with relativism. It is not common to think that those who rightly believe that only novels can be either good or bad novels are thereby committed to relativism. There is no reason to think that if all cultural values are genre based the resulting account is relativistic in any significant way. Williams wonders whether the social dependence thesis implies that once the value emerges it can be applied to the evaluation of events that took place, or practices, institutions, and so on that existed before its emergence. The question is important, but complex, and cannot be fully addressed here. The short, and dogmatically presented, answer is as follows:

[13] The explanation of the genre dependence of many values is briefly repeated below.

1. Formally once a value has emerged it can apply to everything, without temporal restrictions. Many values are, however, genre specific. Only films can be judged as good or bad films, only parties as good or bad parties. Many values that are subject to the special dependence thesis cannot apply to anything that happened or existed before their emergence. The value of poetry emerges with poetry, the value of marriage with the institution of marriage, and so on. Therefore there can be neither good nor bad poems, neither good nor bad marriages before the emergence of the values by which they are judged good or bad.

2. There is an important exception to the generalization about the non-existence of instances to which directly socially dependent values can apply before the emergence of the value. Not infrequently new values arise as a generalization of more specific ones. The notion of a work of art or of literature is more recent than that of a painting or a sculpture, or of a play or a poem. Such new concepts emerge accompanied by new values, leading to a new understanding of the more concrete genres, and their values, to which they apply. Now a poem is an instance of literature, open to comparison with novels, and stories, and plays, to be judged as a work of literature. Such more general values do have instances that existed before they emerged. Those instances were hitherto regarded as belonging to previously existing genres and subject to evaluation by their standards. They still belong to these genres, but now they are also seen as subject to the more general standard of the more general genre. Here we come closest to a retrospective application of a value to the period before its emergence.

3. There is another kind of evaluation, one that does not depend on the existence of instances to the evaluation of which the value in question applies. It may be that the life of people was impoverished, that opportunities for having a fulfilling life were very limited, and so on, because, when they lived, many

values, or some specific ones, had not yet emerged. We pass judgements of this kind regarding the existence or lack of opportunities to take advantage of valuable possible activities and lifestyles. We regret that some art forms, or some sports, are available only to the rich. Judging a life to be impoverished or enriched by the absence or presence of valuable opportunities is indifferent as to whether their absence is due to the non-existence at the time of the values, or of good instances of them, or of opportunities to relate to them in the right way.[14]

4. Finally, there are, of course, various values that do not depend on sustaining social practices, and apply to any suitable object whenever it exists.

None of these observations quite meets Williams's point about 'not having any external moral comment to make' when thinking about the remoter past. He qualifies this remark by noting that it does not apply to all values, and that 'it is at most an option. There is no logical or semantic rule that rules it out that I should condemn the High Middle Ages for not adequately respecting the principles of the First Amendment: it is simply not a very sensible thing to do' (p. 108). I believe that I entirely agree with the sentiment here expressed. Where I feel less certain is whether we agree about the reasons for holding that it is simply not a very sensible thing to do. I am not sure what Williams's reasons are, and am not entirely sure that I understand my own. To be very brief about this let me just say that they seem to me to be a combination of conservative caution, and moral suspicion. The caution is due to a sense that we are all too likely to misunderstand people who live in circumstances very different from our own, and who believe in very different values, or at least in values that they articulate very differently from the way we articulate ours. It is all too easy to miss the meaning of activities, relationships, or practices to people whose values we do not altogether share, too

---

[14] Needless to say, such judgements presuppose that the value in the light of which they are made is available, and applies, either because it falls under the observation above (point 2) or because it is not subject to the special dependence thesis at all.

easy to dismiss them as worthless, too easy to fail to see the good in them, or to overlook that they display values we share in unfamiliar ways. The moral suspicion is of the need people may have to judge others, particularly when the object of the judgement is remote.

VALUES, GENRES, AND NORMATIVITY

The general thesis of the lectures is that by their nature many values depend for their emergence on sustaining social practices, and that most others depend indirectly on social purposes for their existence; appreciation or opportunities to use them depend on such practices, or on values of the first kind. Furthermore, the values successful engagement with which can give meaning to life are, directly or indirectly, socially dependent in these ways. If this is right, then contingent facts affect which values exist and the forms they take. This raises various difficulties, and in the lectures I pointed to and tried to deal with only a few of them. One obvious problem is how is the threat of contradiction avoided. Given that opposing criteria of qualifying as good (say, as a good painting) are to be found, as when we commend one painting for its quietly harmonious character and another for its assertive dissonance, are we not committed to the view that one and the same painting is both good (for its quiet harmony) and bad (for lacking dissonance)? I pointed out that we avoid such contradictions because, when we judge anything as good owing to a value that is subject to the special dependence thesis, we do so in stages. First, we identify a kind to which it belongs, a kind that by its nature or constitution is governed by a particular value (that is, by the standards of excellence for being good of that kind); and, second, we judge the item under consideration good (or bad) to the extent that it is good (or bad) of its kind. This allows us to recognize the existence of values with apparently contradictory criteria.

Korsgaard is right to say that this account leaves many unanswered questions, though we are not always troubled by the same questions. She thinks that 'there is the problem of the bad genre' (p. 69), but I am not sure what the problem is. There would have been a problem had my claim been that every genre is a genre of some value or other. But I did not make such a claim. Rather, I argued that some values (those subject to the special dependence thesis) are genre based.

Korsgaard also asks (regarding the wider genre to which classical architecture may belong): 'What is the wider genre or genus in this case? Western architecture? Decorative architecture? How about "architecture"?' (p. 70). This raises the question of the relations between genres and sub-genres. In the following comments, as in the lectures themselves, I will be concerned only with genres or kinds that are governed by distinct values. So, for example, to establish whether classical buildings belong to decorative architecture, Western architecture or architecture we have to establish first whether the categories in question are evaluative (architecture— perhaps, Western architecture—no, and so on), and then whether the buildings under consideration belong to those that are.

There is no reason to think that either all buildings in the classical style belong to another genre (say decorative architecture) or none does. Some may also be examples of decorative architectures while others may not. Some genres are, however, sub-genres of others, in the sense that necessarily any member of the sub-genre belongs to the genre. Necessarily all historical novels are novels, all comic operas are operas, and so on. I assume that Korsgaard's reference to wider genres is to the genres to which sub-genres refer. Her brief comments suggest the thought that the parent genre provides means of assessing the relative value of instances belonging to different sub-genres. For example, think of two novels. One is a very good detective novel, the second merely a good *Bildungsroman*. Korsgaard's implicit suggestion is that the second may be better than the first if it is a better novel than the first, even though it ranks lower in terms of its sub-genre than the first in its sub-genre. That is not a necessary implication of the views I expressed in the lectures. The standard of excellence of a genre may simply determine that good instances of different sub-genres are good instances of the genre, without providing for their comparative ranking. It all depends on the nature of the genre and its standard of excellence. Nor is there any general reason to think that, given any two items, the one ranked highest in the 'widest', to use Korsgaard's term, genre to which they both belong is the best. There may not be an overall ranking of their value. One may be better in one way, and the other in another way.

These points may help explain the radical pluralistic implications of my view, and the wide-ranging incommensurability of values that is its natural concomitant. But they do not take us to the heart of Korsgaard's disagreement with my views. For me, comparing Korsgaard's view of values and normativity with my own is tantalizingly elusive.[15] There seems to be much that we agree on. But

[15] This is partly because Korsgaard poses the questions to be explored in terms that make sense only if her, or more broadly a constructivist, explanation of normativity is correct. For example, her central question is about the sources of normativity. I do not think that normativity has sources, or rather the metaphor (normativity flowing from its sources) does mischief, and does not help. It is possible to say that my promise is the source of my obligation to do as I promised, or that Congress is the source of our (legal and therefore, in the circumstances, also moral) obligation to pay income tax. But it does not make sense to talk of the source of normativity in general, any more than it makes sense to talk of the sources of properties, or the sources of objects.

I therefore find her analogy of values (on my view) and people misleading. People are not the sources of their own rights, nor of other people's duties towards them (voluntary and legal obligations like promises excepted), any more than great paintings are the sources of the duty to respect them. To be sure, we would not have such a duty if the paintings did not exist, etc., but there is nothing gained from calling them sources of the duties, and doing so invites confusion. I do not believe, as Korsgaard thinks that I do, that values are sources of normative claims. That an object (or event or institution, etc.) possesses an evaluative property makes the proposition that it does true. But that does not make the value a source of any claim any more than the fact that my car has stalled is the source of a claim to that effect.

If, however, constructivism is correct, then normative claims are not like other statements. Other statements that some things have a certain property or stand in a certain relationship are true if they possess the property or stand in the relationship, but normative claims are made true not by things being as they say they are but by the fact that there are valid sources for them, whatever they may be. In attributing to me views about the sources of normative claims, Korsgaard overlooks the fact that talk of 'sources of normativity' has a proper role only within a constructivist approach, and should be introduced only after the validity of that approach has been established.

important disagreements remain. I said that values have no point except to be enjoyed or engaged with by valuers, and that there can be no meaning to the life of valuers, and no point in being a valuer except through the enjoyment of and engagement with values. I also suggested that our grasp of the concepts of value and valuers is inter-dependent, that we cannot fully grasp the one without the other. There are other, closely related, theses about the interdependence of values and valuers. Korsgaard regards this view of the reciprocity and interdependence of valuers and values as unsatisfactory. It leaves my 'theory chasing its own tail' (p. 82), she says. Somehow valuers, people, have the priority in that they are the sources of normativity, and they endow values with normativity. Her view of the priority of valuers is corroborated by an understanding of values that is, in spite of superficial similarities, very different from mine. Let me start with that difference.

Commenting on my remark that the very idea of opera, friend-ship, or the state is a normative idea in that we understand the con-cept of an opera or friendship or the state in part by understanding what a good opera is like, or a good, or successful friendship, or a good state, Korsgaard points out that, if Plato or Aristotle were right, then the same is true of all objects. Perhaps, though I doubt it. I doubt it because I doubt that they had a use for the concept of value that we have today, given that their notion of perfection was bound up with the thought that all objects have a natural tendency to seek their own perfection.[16] Given that I am no expert on the topic, it is lucky for me

[16] Perhaps because Korsgaard overlooks this point, she attributes to me the view that the function of opera is to be a good opera. I doubt that opera has a function (though different operas may have had different functions at different times). If it has a function it is not to be an opera, nor to be a good opera. I am not at all sure what these expressions can mean. Nor, I have to admit, do I understand what is meant by 'stand-ards entirely unique' to a particular object, or of an object 'being perfect of its kind, where its kind is given just by itself'. Perhaps I should add that it is not my view that appreciating sunsets is a social practice. It seems to be some sort of mental activity, or an ability to engage in such activity. However, I do believe that to appreciate the beau-ty of a sunset in the ways we do does presuppose various beliefs (for example, such as exclude the thought that sunsets are signs of the end of the world) and a range of

that we do not have to pursue it, since Plato and Aristotle were wrong, and so, it seems to me, is Korsgaard. It is not the case that 'we understand any kind of thing by understanding what a good or well-functioning thing of its kind is' (p. 77). The simple reason is that regarding many kinds of things it does not make sense to ask what is a good or well-functioning thing of that kind. There are no good or well-functioning stones, or pebbles, or streams, or hail, or snow, or mountains, or stars, or black holes, or electrons, or photons, and so on.

As Korsgaard remarks, 'this may make you feel that we have got derailed somewhere' (p. 79). And indeed it does, and, I believe, we have. It shows that Korsgaard is not really thinking about values at all, and that has far-reaching consequences for the rest of her argument. Of course, hers is not a simple mistake. It is a considered response to a problem. I will try to explain how she is led to her view in stages.

First, some ground clearing. Korsgaard not only attributes to me, but accepts herself, the identity of values with the standards that are constitutive of kinds such that it makes sense to say that there are better or worse instances of that kind, kinds like assassins, chairs, oak trees, and rhododendrons. She also thinks that all kinds are of this type. I have commented on that second claim above, so let us turn to the first.

As I argued in the lectures, where X is a kind that is governed by an intrinsic value (that is, partly constituted by the standards of excellence of that value)[17] we can move from something being a

attitudes to nature whose availability depends on one's familiarity with socially acceptable attitudes to nature, knowledge of aesthetic values, and experience of the ways sunsets featured in culture, their symbolic significance, their portrayal in the arts and literature, their role in romantic love, etc. This does not mean that only experts in all of the above can enjoy sunsets. It merely means that how one enjoys a sunset, how a sunset strikes one intuitively and instantly, depends on one's knowledge and experience of such matters.

[17] I will leave out of consideration here things, persons, etc., which are of value in themselves. See on that topic chapter 4 of my *Value, Respect and Attachment* (Cambridge: Cambridge University Press, 2001).

good X to it being good or of value (a good object, or one of value, etc.) *simpliciter*. A good assassin, as Korsgaard is, of course, aware, is not, in virtue of being an assassin, a good person, or good, or of value, nor is a good hydrangea valuable or of value because it is a good hydrangea. Admittedly all such objects may on occasion be of instrumental value, and some of them—that is, useful artefacts—are normally of instrumental value. Only normally, for the uses for which they were created may cease to exist. Instrumental goods are only contingently so and therefore instances of species that are good if they are instrumental goods are only contingently good or of value. Furthermore,[18] that something is good or of value entails that there is reason to respect it (for example, not to damage it), as well as reason to engage with it in the way appropriate to its value (enjoy looking at it if it is a painting, or listening to it if a piece of music, and so on). The two points (if it is a good X then it is of value, if it is of value there is reason to respect it, and reason to engage with it, or enjoy it) mark the difference between values, even those that are genre based, and kinds constituted in part by standards of excellence in the kind. Not all such kinds satisfy the two conditions, and, therefore, not all of them represent values.

In a way Korsgaard agrees with these points. At least, she agrees that there is no reason to do anything just because it is a good instance of a kind constituted in part by a standard of excellence in the kind. The difficulty is that she tends to think of values as constituted by such intrinsic standards of excellence of any standard-constituted kind. Hence *her* 'values' are not normative—there is no reason to care about them, or to behave in any special way regarding them. Again, I agree with her on that but take it to show that being good of a kind is in itself not being of value, and the relevant kind-constituting standards are not necessarily standards that constitute distinct values or any values at all. For I take values to be inherently normative. And it seems that Korsgaard does not. She says that 'you

---

[18] A point developed in *Value, Respect and Attachment*.

do have reason to care about the values internal to a thing, or perhaps even *have* to care about those values, when the thing is in a certain way yours' (p. 79). Later she explains that we have to care about our health because it is physical excellence and we have a physical nature, and we have to care about cultural excellence because we have a cultural nature. So where do we disagree? First, as already stated, I believe that values are inherently normative—that is, that possessing evaluative properties is inherently related to reasons: we have reasons to pursue actions that possess evaluative properties. Korsgaard treats values as if they are not inherently normative. Second, I believe that, if Korsgaard thinks that having reasons is having reasons to care, then she overstates the weight of reasons, and mischaracterizes them. Third, I do not share her view that we have reasons to care for what is ours, and only for that.

The first point, that values are inherently normative, seems to be a simple and generally known fact about them. While Korsgaard seems to dissent from it, she also seems to think that we should care only for what is of value, and that seems to suggest an intrinsic connection between value and normativity whose nature, in her view, is not clear to me.

The second point is of some importance. I believe that reasonable belief that an action possesses an evaluative property makes its performance intelligible, and if it does possess such a property then, other things being equal, its performance is justified. In other words, I am among those who believe that possession of a value property (that is, the property corresponding to a value, in the way that being beautiful corresponds to the value of beauty) constitutes a presumptively sufficient reason for an action. That does not mean that we have reason to care for everything of value. I agree with Korsgaard that the fact that good Ming pots are beautiful (that is, of value in that way) does not mean that I have reason to care about Ming pots (I will explain this below). That is consistent with the belief that (1) the intrinsic value of actions provides reason to do them, whether or not we care about them, and whether or not we have a presumptively sufficient reason to care about them; and (2) our views about the intrinsic value of actions make it intelligible that we care about what we care about, as well as featuring in the justification of our caring about it, when the caring is justified.

To clarify: caring about an action, or a relationship or pursuit, is more than doing it, or engaging with it. It involves a certain attitude towards it, and it involves letting concern for it play a relatively important role in one's life that includes prioritizing it relative to other matters one has reason for, but that one does not care about (what one must or must not do excluded). Hence, while, by the nature of value and of reason, the value of what we care about is a presumptively sufficient reason to engage in it, it is not necessarily a presumptively sufficient reason to care about it. That is consistent with it being a reason for caring about it, in the sense of necessarily being part of the case for caring about it.

There are cases where we must do things we do not care about. Possibly, in all such cases we should care about them. But caring about them is not a condition without which we have no reason to do them. Furthermore, there are many mundane things we do almost every day simply because they are sensible things to do in the circumstances, even though it would be wrong to say that they connect to anything we care about. At the moment, for example, I sit in a waiting room, waiting for my appointment. I hear the applause of the crowd from a TV in an adjoining room, and, realizing that people there must be watching the Wimbledon men's singles finals, I go there to watch. I do not care about the match or about its result, nor do I care about watching it, or about anything else connected with my action. I am not bored (I could carry on writing this reply), nor have I any other instrumental reason to watch the match. It is simply an (intrinsically) good thing to do, since it is enjoyable. That is an example of how the intrinsic value of things furnishes reasons for action, independently of what we care about and of what we have *special*—that is, presumptively sufficient—reason to care about.

Turning to caring: we need not care about everything of value. But we should not care about things of no value. The value of what we care about gives us reason to care, making our caring intelligible to ourselves and to others, and contributing to its justification when it is justified. Hence intelligible caring presupposes the existence of values, and an account of reasons for caring cannot make an account of values redundant. So far for the second point of possible difference between Korsgaard and me. I do not think that we help ourselves by trying to explain normativity or the role of value by reference to caring and the reasons for it. Reasons for caring are rather special reasons, relating to the role matters can play in our life as a whole. We can explain them by reference to reasons generally, but not the other way round, and we cannot rely on them to capture the way in which all values are normative.

Coming finally to the third point, for Korsgaard having a cultural nature means being collectively, as a species, capable of developing a variety of ways of life, and having the need or the drive to do so. I agree with Korsgaard that there is no point to cultural values unless there are valuers with a cultural nature. I also agree with her that in engaging in cultural activities we should choose good ones rather than bad ones. What determines what are valuable cultural activities and what not? Cultural values. What determines that something is a cultural value, rather than what Korsgaard calls 'a bad value'?

This is not a problem about pluralism. Korsgaard welcomes the existence of a plurality of cultural values. She says:

Could the architectural values grounded in human nature, the values of architecture as such, determine a single absolutely best or right form of, say, dwelling? I do not suppose that any of us will find this *particular* possibility tempting. This is in part because among the things that human beings in fact appreciate in architecture is *variety*. And it is in part because human nature is essentially exploratory ... (p. 72)

It is a puzzle about whether the general nature of culture as a way of life such that people can have various ways of life, and a taste for them, can provide sufficient criteria for the determination of good and bad cultural values. The subject, the fact that we can ask critical questions of ourselves, and so on, cannot provide the answers to the questions we ask. Nor can our taste for variety, and our exploratory nature do that. They are as responsible for values as for what she calls 'bad values'. It all rests on the internal standard of culture, which we should care about because we have a cultural nature. That is where I find difficulty in following Korsgaard's reasoning. I do not understand what is the internal standard of culture, and how it determines which novels, paintings, buildings, operas, string quartets, are good.

How are such matters determined on my view? Here is one way one may be led to Korsgaard's position by criticizing mine: I agree to the obvious—that is, that there are kinds partly constituted by standards of excellence for members of the kind that are not standards of value. I protest that, while on my account cultural values are kind based, not all kinds are kinds of value. Some are kinds of 'bads' and some are indifferent in value. Korsgaard turns to human nature to provide the reasons for caring about certain of these kinds, and therefore about their internal standards, thus providing a test by which we can tell which of them are inherently good, inherently bad, or neither. I availed myself of the distinction but said nothing about how it is determined. We can agree that only if a kind is a kind of value does it follow that if an item is good of that kind it is, *pro tanto*, good. We can agree that if it is good there is reason to engage in it and reason to respect it. These may be so-called formal features of value. They do nothing to tell us what is of value. Korsgaard, whatever the difficulties with her account, at least tries.

I fear that that charge misses the point of my claim that there is mutual dependence between values and valuers and between the concepts of them. It is not so much that my 'theory chases its own tail' as that it denies that between these two one is head and the other tail. As I see it, the search for heads is a search for non-existing shortcuts, a search for secure foundations, secure tests, which enable us to determine what is of value. All value flows from one source, and all we have to do is get to the source and follow the trail. I am not saying that Korsgaard is committed to a foundationalist, linear, view of the process. But I think that the feeling that her, as yet unfulfilled, project of accounting for value and normativity is holding a promise that mine (as yet full of gaps, and so on) does not is due to a yearning for the certainties of foundationalism, and of a linear direction of argument from a single source. Would that it were possible, I may say. For I believe that it is not and we need to employ all the evaluative/normative concepts at our disposal, and resort to many of their essential properties, to understand and establish the nature of any of them, and to establish the nature of what is good or bad. We need to understand the nature of value to understand who can be a valuer, and the nature of valuers to understand what are values, and what can be of value. To establish which kind-constituting standard is the standard of a value, and which is not, we need to deploy arguments that use evaluative premises to establish that the standard is one of a distinct value or that it is not. There is no way to do so without presupposing some value judgements, no test of what are values, or what is valuable that starts with nothing, with no beliefs about values.[19] I said a little about the reasons for that in the lectures, though the argument there is very incomplete.

Perhaps I should add a word about health, given its importance in Korsgaard's comment. At the start of the lectures, to illustrate the significance of the fact that they are only about intrinsic values, I said: 'the value of the means of personal survival, such as food, shelter, good health, is merely instrumental', adding in a footnote: 'That is qua means of survival their value is merely instrumental. Those same things may also have value for other reasons' (p. 16).

Korsgaard is quite right to insist that health is not merely a means of longevity. It is the means for or a necessary precondition of being

---

[19] And of course in this regard evaluative beliefs are like beliefs about material objects and their properties, and like beliefs about psychological properties, etc. There is no test for what there is in 'the material world'. We reason from some beliefs about which material objects there are and what properties they have, etc.

able to engage in many valuable pursuits during our life, however short it may be. She is right that longevity is not a goal in itself, not without the ability to and the prospect of engaging in worthwhile activities. She is also right in saying that we are often rather reckless in our attribution of 'mere instrumental' value to things, and I am no exception. I do not share her doubts about the cogency of the notion, or of the explanation of it given at the beginning of the lectures. I feel that her doubts stem in part from the fact that, when discussing values, she does not have values in mind, but rather kinds constituted by standards and the way instances of them measure up in terms of those standards. But I do agree that we are often careless in failing to distinguish between a thing having instrumental value and it being a precondition of something of value, and so on. Health may be a case in point.

But these are incidental to the main issue in contention between us. Health is one of the conditions enabling us to function well and maximizing our options. The more impaired our health the less able are we to function well, and the fewer are our options. It is in this regard like having all one's limbs, or having skills, or having money. It differs from them, as it is associated with sensations of physical well-being that are intrinsically valuable. As a condition of our ability and of many of our options, it is a condition of both good and ill. It enables us to pursue valuable options, but also to pursue base and evil ones. It is not itself valuable except through its association with the sensations of well-being, and, in as much as it happens to be part of some cultural goal, comparable to body-building. These cases apart, its value depends on the use made of it. It is, therefore, no more than instrumentally valuable, and valuable as a condition of valuable options and abilities.

Korsgaard thinks that it is intrinsically valuable because (1) it is the intrinsic excellence of our physical nature, and (2) our physical nature is ours and we therefore have reason to care about it. I believe that we have reason to foster our health only in as much as we have valuable and realistic goals and pursuits for which it is a precondition.

The issue is not who is right about the explanation of the value of health, but who is right about the sorts of consideration that determine its value. The considerations I adduced are of a familiar type, which we rely on commonly. They apply, not in the details of their content, but in their form, to the value of education, of rest, and much else. I do not suppose that Korsgaard would wish to deny that, whether or not her own argument is sound, they are cogent considerations, and that, whatever else can be said about health, the conclusions they point to are sound as well. But what else can be said about health? Is Korsgaard right that it matters just because we have a physical nature regardless of how that nature relates to our goals and ambitions for our life, that it matters independently of whether we have or should have any goals and ambitions for our life, independently of whether our life has value of any kind at all? I do not think that what she says commits her to such a view. But, if the value of health is conditional on the value of our life, and on the nature of the goals and ambitions we have or should have for our life, then is it not the case that its value is the value of a condition that makes that life, and the realization of those goals and ambitions, possible?

PLURALISM AND LIBERALISM

'Given that buildings have a general function in human life, they must meet certain universal normative standards, standards that enable them to serve those functions, and the result will be universal architectural values. And those values might *conceivably* determine that one genre is better than another' (p. 70). In passages like these Korsgaard appears to think that I claimed that it is necessary that there are many distinct architectural values. In fact I agree with her that it is not necessary that there be such a plurality. It is essential to my position that whether there are any cultural values, and which cultural values exist are contingent matters. Korsgaard seems to acknowledge that the genus-based account of some values contributes to establishing the possibility of value pluralism. Of course, once the possibility of value pluralism is acknowledged, then, given the account of values I advanced, it is a relatively trivial matter to establish that value pluralism is with us. As the comments on the lectures illustrate, what concerns most commentators on value pluralism is not the pluralism of cultural values, the plurality of intrinsically valuable forms of interpersonal relations, of ways of life, or of forms of excellence in the arts, and the like. Their concern is with the plurality of so-called moral values, and of political forms of organization, topics on which I said nothing in the lectures.[20]

Remarking on my view that values come into being at a particular time, and applying it to liberal values,[21] Williams asks

what, on his [i.e. my] view, does that mean for our evaluations of the world before that time? We may recall that ... Raz said that once a value comes into being 'it bears on everything'.... I take it that Raz means that we can apply the value to states of the world before that value existed. It is of course true that we can say evaluative things about earlier societies, and some of them are more sensible than others ... But the present question is more particular: whether on Raz's view the specific values of liberal democracy apply to or 'bear on' earlier societies, such as those of the Middle Ages or the ancient world. ... What are we supposed to say about these people? It can hardly have been a cognitive failure of theirs, not to recognize a value that did not yet exist.... was it a failing of theirs *in terms*

[20] This preoccupation with political values explains, I suspect, Pippin's comment that value pluralism 'is a distinct product of the liberal, democratic, Western, humanistic tradition—and foreign to many others, we most certainly *do* believe it is superior to jingoistic nationalism, the ways of the Taliban, the attacks by Chinese authorities on Falun Gong and so forth' (p. 99). Williams has replied to this contention. Let me just add that what we believe in and the jingoistic nationalists deny is not value pluralism, as explained in the lectures (a view that is far from commanding universal agreement among 'us') but the value of some practices, and the value of tolerating them even if they are mistaken. One need not believe in value pluralism to condemn this kind of jingoistic nationalism, and its repressive practices.

[21] I did not in the lectures, and will not here, address the question what if any are these values. I have discussed these matters elsewhere. Here I only wish to comment on the connection between contemporary liberal thought and the account in my lectures.

of that very value not to have brought that value into existence? Was it a failing of theirs at all that their practices did not accord with these values, as it is a failing in some contemporary societies? Was it even a deficiency of their societies, if it was not yet historically possible for a society to embody these values? If it was not a failing or deficiency of any kind, what is it for the values to apply to them? . . .

There are also real interpretational and ethical questions: how far is it pointful and helpful to discuss earlier states of the world in terms of our more local values? How local are our values? Certainly, as I have said, there is nothing in the nature of the universe or of language to stop one applying one's values in this way. As I have put it in another connection, you can be Kant at the Court of King Arthur if you want to. The question is the extent to which it is reasonable and helpful to do so, or rather gets in the way of understanding; in particular, of understanding how we differ from the past, and hence who we are.   (pp. 112–14)

I have already expressed my agreement with the sentiments expressed in the last paragraph. But I do not think that the social dependence thesis does much to help deal with the question posed by Williams in the first paragraph and that is for the very reason he mentions—that is, once a value exists it applies to everything, including to things that took place before it existed. If liberal values do not apply to the Court of King Arthur, this is because they do not apply universally. To be short, though crude, about it, I would say that they apply only to advanced capitalist societies. To function well, political arrangements, their institutions and principles alike, have to be suited to the social, cultural, and economic conditions of the societies they govern. Otherwise they are liable to cause more harm than good. Liberal principles and institutional arrangements would have been as counterproductive as they are unimaginable in the Middle Ages. To come to this conclusion, no assumption about the time they came into being is needed. The conditions that limit the application of certain principles to appropriate conditions apply, of course, to existing principles.

This is not to say that the repression of gays, or racial discrimination, or female circumcision were ever other than morally abhorrent, but it is typical that we tend to regard values or principles whose application is not restricted to favourable social, cultural, or economic conditions as moral rather than political. Be that as it may, without going into detailed examination of this principle or that value, all one can say is that by and large my thesis about the temporal and contingent element in values parallels and chimes in its practical implications with the fact that political principles and institutions are contingently suitable to specific conditions of human societies.[22] It is not, however, the basis for such conclusions.

All this is in principle consistent with thinking that liberal principles and institutions, or any others, are superior to all rival political principles and institutions. It is possible to hold that, and therefore maintain that, if they can bear their beneficial fruits only under certain conditions, it is important to bring about those conditions, and so on. But, 'I find this very hard to believe', to quote Williams, and for the very reasons he gives in his comment: 'The peculiarity of human beings is their capacity and need to live under culture, and I do not see how it could be that this capacity and need, properly understood, will reveal that human beings are really "meant to" live under one fairly specific form of culture, that of liberal modernity' (p. 115–16),[23]

---

[22] That the suitability of political arrangements is determined by other social factors does not deny, of course, that existing political arrangements have a deep influence on other aspects of social life. I do not hold the view that political principles and values are some sort of 'superstructure', made suitable by some 'base', without having causal effects on the character of the existing 'base'.

[23] Williams adds: 'Underlying this is a more general issue of principle. If there is such a thing as an essential nature of human beings, there is only one way in which it can rule anything out—by making it impossible. If it has failed to rule it out in that way, it cannot try to catch up by sending normative signals' (p. 116). This is, however, less clear if one accepts the possibility that there are normative aspects of human nature. This would make it possible for some essential human features to send 'the normative signals' by which other matters may be judged. Like him, I do not think that this is much help in singling out preferred forms of culture. The one qualification I would enter is that human nature may mark some matters, like susceptibility to pain and its potential consequences, or the importance of sex to human experience, that do send normative signals as to the fact that some aspects of cultures are repressive. These enable us to condemn some aspects of all human societies known to us.

Pippin was alone among the commentators in remarking on my contention regarding interpretation and underdetermination. Among other things he observes that

Both defenders and opponents of affirmative action may be responding to a general underdetermination in the way our social practices sustain the value of, guide interpretations of, rights protection, or fair social entitlement, a value they both agree on. But the fact that they agree on the absolute value of rights protection is largely irrelevant when compared with the depth of their disagreement, and the unavoidability of some decision. Our suspicion that reason is incapable of ever resolving the dispute in favour of one side or the other (that the matter is therefore essentially a political contestation, a struggle for power) remains a genuine anxiety. (p. 101)

I may not have put the matter in precisely these terms, but essentially we agree here. I share Pippin's awareness of the limits of reason, and one of the aims of establishing its power and credentials is to establish where its writ does not run. I do not share his apprehension of loss of faith in philosophy given its inability to solve disputes such as the one he alludes to above. I do not think that philosophy has all that much to contribute to the solution of such disputes. It is a fallacy, encouraged by some of the most successful recent writers in political philosophy, that philosophy can out of its own resources do much to solve deep social divisions and social problems.

But nor do I believe that that means that appeal to values, principles, and reasoned arguments has nothing to do with these disputes. On the contrary, the disputes cannot take place in anything like the form they do but for their appeal to values and principles. The very underdetermined rights, principles, and values, which fail to resolve the disputes, frame them, define their terms, and the nature of the aspirations of the rival parties. Nor is the fact that the issues are underdetermined by values show that the disputes are no more than a naked power struggle, and the appeal to reasons a mere self-serving rationalization. It is true that the parties are rarely clear about the philosophical presuppositions of their claims, but that is not unique to disputes where reason underdetermines the issue. What matters is that the rival parties advance ideals, representing different ways in which values can be implemented, or developed. They appeal to the public's imagination, trying to convince it to opt for their vision and against its rivals. It is not a process with a unique rational outcome. But it is not one where values and reasons play no role.

We can compare it to two friends debating the relative merits of two films, neither of which is better than the other, but where each friend strongly likes one and dislikes the other. (It is perfectly all right not to like things of value, provided one is not basing the dislike on false beliefs.) They like what they like for good reasons (let us assume) and they try to show the other how attractive is their favourite film by invoking those reasons. That is one way in which people come to develop a taste for one style or another, in films, clothes, friendship, and much else—not because it is rationally superior to others, but because it appeals to one, hopefully for good reasons, more than alternatives that have no lesser reasons in their favour. Our responses to rival political ideals or policies are often similar. That is, often there are reasons for both ideals and neither is better than the other. Some of us will be attracted to one of the ideals, while others are attracted to their rivals. We try to make others share our taste by presenting the ideals or policies to them in ways that display their attractions, make them more visible, more palpable to those who as yet do not share our preferences.

In the lectures I highlighted a somewhat different, though related, manifestation of underdetermination by reason. Such under-determination, I said, often manifests itself in the fact that there are rival interpretations of *common* ideals none of which is superior to the others. Different interpretations would support somewhat different courses of action, somewhat different institutional arrange-ments, and so on. But neither can be said to be the best. In such cases, it is evident that reason plays a crucial role in the political advocacy of the rival camps, for their views, being interpretations of common ideals, cannot even be understood except by understanding the values that underlie these ideals, and the way they play their role in the different interpretations of them.

It is important that we should not exaggerate what we can establish by force of reason, and that we should realize that one crucial test of a satisfactory constitution is that it allows channels for causes to be promoted for good decisive reasons, and another is that it allows channels for causes to be promoted, and for reasonable distributive decisions to be made, because they represent people's preferences, which, though based on reasons, are not superior to some alternatives that they could have opted for, and that others in the population prefer.

Index

CPSIA information can be obtained at www.ICGtesting.com
Printed in the USA
BVOW10s1416301113

337776BV00008B/115/A